TINA SATTER

Seagull (Thinking of you)

with Away Uniform and FAMILY

53rd State Press
Brooklyn, New York

53SP 18
December 2013

ISBN no. 978-0-9857577-7-9
Library of Congress Control no. 2013956283

53rdstatepress.org

For my mum, Helen.

Amuse-bouche

You know what a play is, right?

(I mean…)

We all do.

But what if a play could be a bunch of scenes that were sort of the same only not, and didn't really add up to a story or anything but just drifted along, and the scenes were all short and small and borderline random, so sometimes it seemed like nothing much was really happening—except it was?

Like, for example…

"Chekhov didn't really care about plot in an overarching sense. It was just a framework to set up those obscured, simmering, often devastating moments between lovers, crushes, family, acquaintances—those micro-moments that are the action for him. Where he created a landscape and a setting. Where the real plot was unfolding for him. Microplots like that work for me. They feel so much more realistic to how things actually go. I've never cared about plot in a traditional way, or known how to care about it, or wanted to do it right.… I am interested in the possibilities in the small things that are actually the big things, the female things, the queer things. The things we don't know are queer, seen through slightly or very off eyes. To go under and around and next to things we know, and unearth the odd corners, the secret palpitating heart, the perfect stupidness that is actually the amazingness, and the humor and awkwardness inherent to the attempt of live performance. Because if not here [i.e., on the stage], where?"

And what if all the people in the play turned out to be members of some weird community, like a dysfunctional family or a field hockey team? And they all had secrets from each other and the secrets were different for each person, and everyone knew that everyone else had secrets, too, and they even sometimes tried to tell them? But they never quite did?

You know....?

"There are just so many things where you feel like your family is the darkest most fucked up group of people but then you're like, laughing about it and aware of the edges of love. I'm always interested in those kinds of things with groups of people. I think I'm a little too interested in them. They're filled with so much fucking fucked up love. And I think I'm sort of obsessed with that fucked up love actually. It's these dynamics of people who know a space really well and know each other really well but within this specific set-up. I wanted to look at the small ways these characters bounce off each other in this really small container—trying to communicate with each other or avoiding communicating with each other."

And what if all the actors in the play were always the same? And they all played people who either had a song or a dance or an act or some routine they kept rehearsing or doing or just talking about all the time for no good reason?

I mean…

"Since we're never really dealing with typical psychological stakes in Half Stradde work, the performers—who are all incredible performers and wonderful friends—their raw personalities become a layer of the narrative in an essential and physical way. I love this tension—it's my favorite thing about seeing any work, I think. When it hits this perfect tight looseness: where you see the rigor of what has been worked on and planned, inhabited by these real people, that you probably love, actually being themselves within this frame to make something we've never seen before, that holds. "

And what if all the people in the play were girls, even the ones that weren't, and they all had this weird coded, adolescent teenage girlspeak that was some kind of weird adolescent girl magic?

What if…

"I just want to make the play that's in my heart. 'Cause my heart's fucked up and complicated like anyone's. But sometimes I want to make that play and stage it there. Like, right there. On a tiny stage inside my heart. But I know that's impossible."

— Jeffrey M. Jones

"Schmoetics (A Poetics Talk by Tina Satter)," Prelude.12, CUNY, October 3, 2012

Tina Satter, in an interview with Katherine Cooper, "BOMBlog," BOMB Magazine, November 5, 2013

"Schmoetics"

Tina Satter, in "Theatre is such a Hustle," MASSMoCa, Web. December 6, 2012

Tina Satter, interview with Sarah LaDuke, Northeast Public Radio, December 12, 2012

"Schmoetics"

Things You Wrote That I Didn't Always Understand

At the end of Act 2 in Chekhov's *The Seagull*, Nina Zarechnaya, a young wannabe actress, steps to the edge of the stage and says, "I'm dreaming." On the heels of her first serious encounter with the established writer and melancholic, Trigorin, she has every reason to be enthusiastic—the shit of her life hasn't hit the fan yet. Or maybe it has, a little—broody, misguided Treplev throwing a dead bird at her feet and threatening to kill himself after one bad show might constitute some serious shit—but all that slips away in the presence of the aspirational: art embodied by a heroic single-mindedness. And Nina knows, in the instant she declares to Boris all she would sacrifice to be in his shoes, what she wants to do and be: an artist. On the precipice of a subversive self-discovery, she articulates a sad but liberating and intrinsically queer value: that the self is perhaps never to be discovered, but always to be made, and the way she chooses to go about her making is her life. I think this sentiment beautifully describes the project of my friend and art partner Tina Satter, a writer constantly reminding me that we must treat and observe surface with as much care as we afford depth.

Seagull (Thinking of you), Tina's illuminating and elliptical response to Chekhov, finds its inspiration in the performance of Nina's impassioned rhetoric and then complicates the affair by taking her adolescent utterance at face value and radically running with the proposal. I'm dreaming: darker than a fangirl's squeal, but just as powerful a frequency. Tina endows the line with the full weight of its implication, imagining a new world order, fluid and fantastic, where masculine presence is collapsed, in the single character of Peter/Dorn/Trigorin, to make new space for Nina's machinations, from imagining Arkadina as the woman cast to play her in the biopic of her life to intimate, existential chats with Masha. Tina shatters the expectations of adaptation and from these shards creates a dazzling mosaic of feminine agency: sharp, jagged, dangerous, and, most importantly, "shining."

Thankfully, Tina has a sense of humor, or a reconfiguring like this might quickly collapse under the strain of sentimentality and become a more familiar feminist revisionism, easier to pin down for its empowering action, while doing nothing to revitalize the terms of the conversation. Tina's protagonists *make themselves* like no others I am familiar with in our theater today, their speech unapologetically defiant, insular, myopic, aesthetically aware and hyper-feminized—think of those "amateur" detectives of Susan Glaspell's *Trifles*, if they'd had the good sense to tell everyone to "Fuck off" and started their own play. Lives littered with Diet Coke cans, precious stuffed seals, bottles of nail polish, nonsense sing-a-longs about nothing and everything. Some say God is in the details, Tina might say it's in the vagaries. (If she has made just one major contribution to twenty-first century drama, it may be the complete re-invigoration of the '90s adolescent cry "Whatever.")

A peer of the two Richards (Foreman and Maxwell) in her affections for stillness and prosaic encounter, a protégé of Wellmanian "weirdness," a disciple of the awe-inspiring Fornes, Tina's sensibility is the product of much close study and good reading. And even better watching, perhaps. I remember, vividly, when I was 24 and we had just started working together on a collaboration for the Incubator Arts

Project Short Form series, how she taught me, by example, how to ride the subway properly, with my eyes and ears open like a writer, how to find volumes of joy in imperceptible gestures, to see the ever-present joke before it had been written. The first monologue she ever wrote for me, a kernel that grew into 2008's *The Knockout Blow* was from the perspective of a devastated werewolf whom no one blinks at, grieving on a train, alienated by form and feeling.

Tina ingests pop culture without pretense. Her work owes as much to the avant performance pantheon as it does to Mike Kelley's re-staged and meticulously crafted traumas, Alex Bag's insouciant video art, the cult personality of Chloe Sevigny, the wunderkind efforts of *Rookie Mag*'s Tavi Gevinson and the ethos of the New Narrative school (one of our first bonding experiences was swapping Chris Kraus novels).

Magical and infuriating in their delicious specificity, consider a smattering of potential questions inspired by a first read of these plays: *How did the ladies of* FAMILY's *archipelago get ahold of Rudolf Nureyev's sperm? What about this "fertilizer shit"* Away Uniform'*s JayJay keeps snorting up his ass? When will Peter and the rest of The Seagull Family Players finally get to use the small satchel?* Sublimely ridiculous, these are questions without answers—made-up, make-believe, reminiscent of the ways children first learn how to amuse themselves, stealing words and ideas like naïve sponges, absorbing them to make something wild and new and "wrong."

Uninterested in the tedium of fixed, metaphorically endowed objects, Tina's work re-animates the ephemeral in sustained variation. She proposes language, alternately base and poetic, as the holy, throbbing frame necessary for creating a heightened consciousness of wonder and bewilderment. When she is most vulnerably abstract, I am reminded of the feeling I had when I visited the Rothko Chapel for the first time, or finding myself blessedly alone in front of a Pollock painting—calm, patient beyond knowing, present and transformed by that awareness of my presence. Think of Janet Cardiff's gorgeous perimeter of speakers in her installation *The Forty Part Mortet*, each speaker showcasing a single voice in a choir performing a sacred Renaissance-era composition, inviting us to be in the midst of a transcendent force field. Cardiff explains: "I am interested in how sound may physically construct a space in a sculptural way and how a viewer may choose a path through this physical yet virtual space." Tina's words, like these sounds, similarly make this space for a kind of making.

And in honor of her work, I won't try to explain that sentence or anything else to you anymore, but I will leave you with a very lovely poem she wrote, excerpted from one of the first plays she ever brought to our shared workshop at Brooklyn College, the yet unproduced *ENNUI ISN'T SADNESS; AND OTHER THINGS YOU WROTE THAT I DIDN'T ALWAYS UNDERSTAND*. It's a play veiled as a eulogy for a young girl named Joanie whom nobody quite understood, but was best remembered for being a weirdo, an artist and a person who "loved being inspired" and could find inspiration where others could not. Performing for Tina over the last six years, this title has come to epitomize my relationship to embodying her words, the things that are sometimes incomprehensible to me, but always important and real and alive.

—Jess Barbagallo

Still to Come

There was a time and a place.
When the clouds were real.
And the sky was glass.
And everyone knew that nothing and everything would always mean something.
And this revelation, this news, passed through the land – the news was harkened in the antennas of slow-moving slugs, in the soft under feathers of all birds, in the long lashes of a pachyderm so that in Africa, in Asia, in the ocean and at home, it was unanimously known that a crystallized thought of interminable, fleeting consciousness had come and gone.
And once the animals and the peoples and the messages on high had been delivered it was time to turn around and do the other work.
The deciphering of love and loss that having been writ so small was now so vast.
And like an ark of subterranean mystics getting ready to dock in the real world, no one knew what lay ashore on this shimmering ground.

Seagull
(Thinking of you)

Characters:

Nina, a young woman who wants to be an actress

Masha, a young woman who loves Treplov

Treplov, a young man who wants to be a playwright and is in love with Nina

Arkadina, an actress and Treplov's mother

Peter, an actor (who also takes on the role of Trigorin, a novelist who Arkadina loves)

Polina, the stage manager

Russian Language in the Play / Phonetics and Energy

In parts of the play, the performers are called on to speak Russian. The performers from the original production learned to speak the Russian lines phonetically and it became a critical rhythm of the scenes it was used in, so that is how it is noted in this text – written out phonetically, followed in most instances by its English translation in parentheses. In An Opening Moment and Big Russian Scene in Russian, in addition to set language, the performers spoke various Russian lines on the fly depending on the flow of the scene show to show. Those moments are described here in English for more clarity instead of entirely transcribed in phonetic Russian. In those scenes the rhythm of the language in its emotional arc and hearing the essence of Russian paired with the flow of the performers' energy and movement is most important, as opposed to having completely perfected spoken Russian.

Russian Folk Metal in This Play

The original score for this play was inspired by and drew from the Russian neo-pagan folk metal band, Arkona. This hard and folk-inflected sound as the musical baseline is important to consider because it functions as the dark under-edge of the particular Chekhovian universe created in this play. Accordingly, the intensity of music is noted in several stage directions where it feels particularly relevant for those moments.

AN OPENING MOMENT

The light subtly changes in the space as the play starts, setting the tone that carries throughout the play for the feeling of a place that is glowing and dimming from within and outside itself on a rhythm tied to the energies of the group of people inhabiting it.

At the top of the play, as the light shifts to a brighter, but softened pink look, there is also light dialogic sound – birds, doorknobs, feet on floor – that is musical.

A final horse neigh is followed by the six performers entering the stage speaking low in Russian to each other as needed to move through the following sequence:

Polina enters and walks down far stage left. Entering right behind her is Masha who speaks a passing greeting to Polina, then exits.

Nina speaks to Arkadina about a role she is working on. Arkadina listens and offers advice.

Peter walks in working on his lines. Arkadina sees Peter. Nina looks up, sees Peter, returns to her conversation with Arkadina.

Treplov walks in. Masha comes back in, adjusting part of her outfit. She sees Treplov, goes to speak to him, and asks if he thinks she should wear a side ponytail for her audition. Treplov is fairly uninterested in Masha's hair dilemma. Masha expresses her annoyance and walks away.

Masha then tries to talk to Nina. Nina sees her, but keeps talking to Arkadina as she is excited to have time alone with her. Treplov walks over, says hi to Nina too. Nina keeps talking to Arkadina.

Masha tries to speak to Nina again. Treplov tries again too. Arkadina then does start to talk to Masha, sort of to her son, Treplov.

Upset at losing Arkadina's undivided attention, Nina snaps at all of them and moves away.

As the light fades to a darker blue, the entire group stops, raises their left hand and does a synchronized movement together that they repeat several times, bringing their right hand up to their left, then down and snapping.

The movement and tone now feels more deliberate and connected.

Polina and Masha move downstage left facing directly out to the audience.

They have a short conversation in Russian in which Masha laments that everything is shitty and there is no hope. She offers a drag of her cigarette to Polina who declines.

The soundscape builds underneath their speaking. As it builds to its crescendo and their conversation ends, the performers move together into different groupings, no longer speaking at all, until the following scenes start.

Treplov exits. The others remain. The darker blue has faded up to a more neutral state.

POLINA, PETER and ARKADINA

All three stand next to each other looking straight out at the audience. Polina is in the middle with Peter to her right, Arkadina to her left.

POLINA: *(To Arkadina.)* Here's your small satchel for Scene 3. *(To Peter.)* Did you retrieve the fur coverlet?

PETER: Which coverlet?

POLINA: The fur coverlet.

PETER: The fur coverlet. Yes. Am I still in that section then?

POLINA: I haven't heard otherwise.

They exit.

NINA and MASHA

Nina and Masha stand shoulder to shoulder looking straight out at the audience.

MASHA: What?

NINA: Nothing.

MASHA: I saw you yesterday. Doing that.

NINA: Doing what?

MASHA: Sitting around. Acting like you were, like, acting. Like channeling pleasure. Or something.

Masha slowly starts to fall to her left, Nina pinches her right arm and brings her back up to standing.

NINA: What are you going to do about it?

Masha turns and walks directly stage right with one foot in front of the other, and does a weird look out towards – but not at – the audience.

MASHA: I think you might be looking at it.

Treplov enters upstage from behind them and drops the book he is distractedly reading. Nina and Masha turn towards him at the sound of the book hitting the floor.

The music builds to the pre-scene height as the characters move into the first scene below.

Music drops out.

ARKADINA, MASHA, POLINA and TREPLOV

Polina, Arkadina, and Treplov sit working.

Masha enters.

MASHA: I can't find the kettle.

ARKADINA: It's by the mousepack.

Masha stands there.

Next to the samovar.

Pause.

TREPLOV: I know where the kettle is. I brought it into the barn.

ARKADINA: What?

TREPLOV: Nina had a blister.

They all look at Treplov.

MASHA: *(Barely audible, under her breath.)* Where?

Pause.

TREPLOV: *(Standing up.)* But, Mum. I can't find my wrist-watch.

ARKADINA: Did you look under the pile of rugs?

TREPLOV: Yes.

ARKADINA: Dammit. Well, I don't know.

TREPLOV: Everyone leave me alone! *(Exits. Followed immediately by Masha.)*

ARKADINA: *(To Polina.)* Do you know what it feels like to know you are a bad actor? Do you know that feeling? I didn't know what to do with my hands, or how to move, I had no control of my voice.

POLINA: Yes, I do know. Raising children is no picnic. Control goes out with the ants.

ARKADINA: I'm better now. I figured out if it was something I can still do and I came out on the other side. And I can be passionate. And those eyes. I can feel very beautiful when I'm up here. My spirit. And, I understand now, that whether I am here onstage, or, you're there… working… the most important thing isn't fame, or glory, or anything you might hope for in your deepest heart. It's the ability to survive. To keep moving, and drink your coffee, and squench down anything else you want. And I might be quite crazy, but it could be a lot worse. I have never been arrested, you know.

Nina enters.

POLINA: I spent three years in the Gulag. And, you do have friends there too, at the end of the day.

Treplov and Masha re-enter.

MASHA: *(To Nina.)* Grab your cloak, we gotta boogie. *(To Treplov.)* Are you coming?

TREPLOV: It's my play.

Polina puts the cloak on Nina, kisses both her cheeks.

ARKADINA: *(Under her breath, exiting.)* What's that smell?

TREPLOV: See you Mum.

Peter enters.

PETER: I can't find my hairpiece. *(To Masha.)* You on book today?

MASHA: Yes. It's what I will do until I die. And we will die.

Masha and Treplov exit.

PETER and NINA

Nina moves through stiff ballet poses and whispers instruction to herself. She holds a small boom box and a branch of flowers.

PETER: Vera.

NINA: *(Very under her breath.)* It's Nina. *(Regular tone.)* I can't talk.

PETER: Shut up.

NINA: No. I'm serious. I can't talk.

PETER: I hate you. You're the worst niece a man could have.

NINA: Stop it. I can't warm up like this, what scene are you doing anyways? I need my script. Hold on. Unhhh. Shit. Where's my script?

PETER: I'm not trying to run lines. What I'm saying is/

NINA: Why are you doing this? I'm losing my voice. I feel like I'm not going to be able go on. Susie spilled my peppermint tea – and does it look like I'm wearing too much foundation?

PETER: I'm telling you separately from the parts we play in the play, that I think I hate you. And – you are an absolutely awful niece.

Long pause.

Nina stares at Peter while collecting her thoughts. She looks to the side. She learns over and turns on the boom box. The song "Only You" by Yaz begins to play. Nina sings a section of it in Russian:

Glyadyah iz ahknah veeshye
Eta kak istoriya lyoobve
Tee menyah sleeshish?

[Looking from a window above
It's like a story of love
Can you hear me?]

Peter bends down and turns off the boom box from where he is standing. He exits.

NINA RUNNING LINES WITH TREPLOV

Treplov enters.

TREPLOV: Ready?

NINA: When you are.

Nina touches Treplov's shoulder. Treplov looks at Nina.

TREPLOV: Seriously. Stop sexualizing me. It puts me off. I can't work like this.

NINA: Eww. Okay.

Nina goes to center stage to speak. Treplov takes his glasses out of his fur fanny pack, places them on his face, and sits down holding a script.

Just as Nina is about to begin, Arkadina enters, removes Treplov's white jean jacket for him and exits the scene.

Nina begins to run her lines.

NINA: "If I was a writer like you, I would give my entire"/

TREPLOV: No. Start again.

NINA: "If I was a writer like you, I would give my whole life over to my fans. I would endure the disapproval of my family, the poverty, the – the, the *(Trying to remember.)*

TREPLOV: ...the disappointments.

NINA: Yes! The disappointments. *(Repeats.)* "If I was a writer like you, I would endure the disapproval of my family, the poverty, the disappointments."

Nina goes to Treplov and leans in to double-check her lines in the script. Treplov does a weird hair touch to her high bun. She doesn't notice and returns center to begin the monologue again.

NINA: *(Poised to deliver the monologue, then breaks.)* ...I don't even care about myself, or another person, or myself even... you know. I don't! And that feeling is so empty that it's actually like then I can see it. And then almost literally get my arms around it. *(Treplov walks to her.)* No, no, god! I am trying to explain to you… fuck it. More than trying. It's happening.

Pause.

Treplov looks at Nina, then far out over the audience.

TREPLOV: There goes Nina Zarechnaya, star of Melikhova Farm…

Nina looks back at Treplov. They hold a gaze.

NINA: Did you bring that cell phone?

Treplov hands Nina a cell phone and exits.

NINA and ARKADINA

Nina enters and sits. Arkadina stands downstage of her.

ARKADINA: Your eyes look a little like they were crying… that's not good.

NINA: It's just… I'm still catching my breath. I have to leave in half an hour – I lost my other cell phone – we'd better hurry. You mustn't keep me any later, for God's sake. My father doesn't know I'm here.

ARKADINA: Actually it's time to begin, we should call the others.

NINA: My father and his wife won't let me come here. They say you're all a bunch of bohemians. *(Standing.)* They're afraid I'll become an actress. But. My heart is full of you.

ARKADINA: We're alone.

Arkadina moves to Nina.

NINA: I don't know.

ARKADINA: It's fine.

They kiss quite intimately.

NINA: What kind of tree is that?

ARKADINA: Elm.

NINA: The light is weird in here.

ARKADINA: It's that time of day. Don't leave early.

NINA: It's impossible.

ARKADINA: I'll stand outside your window all night long and look up at your room from the street.

NINA: Don't.

ARKADINA: I love you.

NINA: Shhh. *(She steps away from Arkadina.)* Your play is hard to act. There's no live people in it.

ARKADINA: Live people. I don't want to represent life as it is, or even as it should be, but how it appears underneath.

NINA: Nothing really happens in your play either, it's all talk. And. I always think that plays should have love in them.

Pause.

Nina bows and exits.

Arkadina remains center, looking out.

TREPLOV and ARKADINA

Treplov enters as Arkadina remains center.

TREPLOV: Mum. Mum. What are you doing? Did you see the new section I wrote? I think it's really strange and/

ARKADINA: These lines, like here. *(Touching her face.)* Do you see them?

TREPLOV: What are you talking about? You never ask me things like that.

ARKADINA: Forget it.

TREPLOV: You're weird. *(Pause.)* It's usually more like, "What should we have for dinner?" "Did you call the troika?" "Why would you leave a loaded baked potato in the kitchen if we're out of sour cream?" "Do you have any friends?"... you know, that sort of thing.

ARKADINA: *(Distracted.)* What? I didn't hear you. Can you say that again?

TREPLOV: Did you call the troika? Why would you leave a loaded baked potato in the kitchen? If we're out of sour cream. Do you have any friends? *(Pause.)* You know.

Masha skateboards across upstage accompanied by Russian folk metal. As she skates off stage right, the lights glow bright.

INTO THE SITTING ROOM/GARDEN

Masha and Nina enter together. Polina is sitting center sewing. They join her.

Treplov enters shortly after and sits at their feet writing in his journal.

MASHA: I'm not trying to be annoying. You just may not know what it's like to have a partner or whatever you want to call it around for years who gets on every single one of your nerves. Every thread. I don't know. Maybe that is also something other people have a relationship too. I mean, obviously it is. It's part of why life can be so boring. I mean, it turns out when you tell someone something, they have the exact same dumb old ideas to talk about with you – just from their perspective.

Arkadina and Peter enter speaking softly to each other in Russian.

Nina exits, stopping to whisper something in Russian to Treplov as she goes.

Masha and Arkadina greet each other in Russian briefly.

ARKADINA: *(To Masha.)* Stand up. Stand next to me. You're twenty-two, and I'm almost a widow's age. Peter, who looks younger?

PETER: You do. Of course.

ARKADINA: You see, and why? I work, I feel things passionately, I'm always a part of the world. You sit here like a lump, you're not really living. I have one rule: don't think about tomorrow. I never think about old age, or death. What will be, will be.

MASHA: *(Walking to downstage edge.)* I feel like I was born eons ago. My whole life trails behind me like an enormous train that is dragging from my dress. Sometimes I don't know why I bother. *(Returning to sit.)* Anyways, it's all crazy. I need to snap out of it *(she slaps her face)*, and get my shit together.

ARKADINA: What's more, I keep myself in tune, as they say, and this is why I've kept my looks, because I've never been slatternly, never let myself go, like others I could mention. I can still play 15, you know.

Nina returns.

PETER: *(To Nina.)* Well. Do you think we're finally happy to-day?

NINA: *(To Peter.)* I'm so happy. *(To Arkadina.)* I'm all yours today.

Nina, Arkadina, and Peter exit.

TREPLOV, MASHA and POLINA

Polina remains sitting. Masha circles upstage of Polina and then returns to center.

MASHA: What's she so good at? Nina. You know.

TREPLOV: She's quite good at dying beautifully.

POLINA: 'Tis true. *(Exits.)*

MASHA: Like this? *(Does a fake die which concludes with her falling dead weight towards Treplov. Treplov catches her.)*

TREPLOV: Cut it out. You need to know what you're talking about to be good at it.

MASHA: Not true at all.

Treplov picks up Masha's skateboard and hands it to her.

TREPLOV: I know I messed up. I just fucked up in terms of really being a present person when you needed it. But, it was like I couldn't always be that thing.

They start to slow dance.

MASHA: Try!

TREPLOV: I was just so flawed I made it worse.

MASHA: You have to try and fix it. You have to try to fix it. Please. *(She falls backwards to the ground in a static pleading gesture.)*

TREPLOV: But, how can I fix it. How can I fix it? I did that. All this is what's here.

PETER and POLINA

Peter and Polina stand downstage left looking out.

POLINA: *(To Peter.)* I have an idea. We could… kiss. But then, we can't talk for at least a week or even two. *(Pause.)* It's like a two-part idea.

PETER: Okay.

They kiss. Music swells.

PASHA CHADIN

Nina, Peter, and Arkadina walk towards the chairs set center. Nina and Peter are reminiscing. Polina eventually joins upstage. Masha spies on the group from the upstage curtains, eventually getting closer.

NINA: …In 1873, she was at the fair at Poltava, and she was simply amazing. It was sheer ecstasy.

Nina and Peter sit.

PETER: Really brilliant.

NINA: Whatever happened to that comedian, Pavel Chadin? No one could compare with his Rasplyuev, far better than Sadovsky's performance, I swear, dear woman.

PETER: Where is he now?

ARKADINA: You're always asking about these old dinosaurs. How should I know? *(Sits.)*

NINA: Good old Pasha Chadin.

PETER: They don't make them like that anymore. *(Treplov enters and walks downstage.)* The theater is not what it used to be.

NINA: *(Looking at Treplov.)* Once there were huge oaks, now only the stumps remain.

TREPLOV: Hogwash. There may be fewer shining lights these days, I'll grant you that – but some of those stumps do really nuanced work. They're more in themselves. Channeling charisma – you know – in a really fascinating way. It's a new kind of acting.

NINA: Huh. I'm not sure I know what you're talking about. But, regardless, I think I couldn't agree less. Of course, it's a matter of taste.

Pause.

PETER: And if you can't say something nice about the dead don't say anything at all, right.

ARKADINA: Here. *(Standing up, moving downstage.)* Look. I'm going to try to pretend I've never felt more alive... *(Pretends she has never felt more alive.)* And... scene.

The others clap vigorously.

All exit except Nina and Masha, and Polina who sits and sews for a bit more and then leaves during the following scene.

NINA and MASHA

Nina pulls Masha forward to the very edge of the stage.

NINA: When I go out there, why can't it feel like? Why can't it feel like we don't have to add on any layer? That we're just like/

MASHA: Shining?

NINA: Yes, shining!

MASHA: Like your hair – which you know is perfect.

NINA: So is yours!

MASHA: But it doesn't matter, listen, listen, your hair, and the parts underneath, the connectors into your inside parts – those are like gleaming out – and that's what everyone can see – and then, you know? Come on, do you know?

NINA: Yes. Maybe it is just like when I stood up that one day in the dacha, I was holding Greenbean, the smallest puppy in the batch, and we were leaving for the country, and I could feel my feet, in those little Russian brown boots/

MASHA: Made on this soil?

NINA: Yes, oh my god, shut up. Yes, made here. And I could feel my feet went to my ankles, up my legs, this was my waist, my shoulders, and my eyes, and I could feel that I was bigger than what used to be around me. That this was me, standing there, like it was real and, um, god, do you know what I'm saying?

MASHA: I think so, I think I do.

NINA: But it felt, like the moment of knowing, of/

MASHA: Realizing?

NINA: Yes. I guess so. Of realizing or something that I had actually grown *(makes a chopping mark up her arm)*, that I stood on the earth, that I was taller than I used to be, that/

MASHA: So some things looked smaller.

NINA: Yes... and that... and that... just that then.

MASHA: I think that I know, Nina.

Nina steps forward. Masha follows.

NINA: Greenbean had really greasy fur.

MASHA: Eww, I know. Small dogs often have gross fur.

Pause.

NINA: I want the toughest dog ever.

Masha steps next to Nina.

MASHA: I'll be that. I'll be a really good actor too.

NINA: Then get on your hands and knees and stay there. *(Masha begins to lower herself to the ground.)* And follow me around. *(Masha is now on all fours beside Nina.)* But don't be weird about it. *(Pause.)* And if you see my stepmother, grrrrr.

Both girls growl. Then stand and exit upstage together as the folk metal music rises up.

POLINA and PETER Hairblowing Interlude

Occurs under a loud sound cue and music. Polina asks Peter to blow in her hair, then blows in his. Treplov walks in. They also blow in his hair. They remain doing this until Arkadina enters and interrupts saying "Lock the doors" under the music.

PETER and ARKADINA (as Treplov and Nina)

All exit except for Peter. Arkadina remains.

ARKADINA: Lock the doors. *(Pause.)* Let me look at you. It's warm here. This used to be a sitting room. Do I look different?

PETER: You're thinner. You're eyes look big.

ARKADINA: I thought you hated me. I dreamed every night that you looked right at me and didn't recognize me. God. I've come here so many times since I got back. To your place so many times. But I couldn't come in. Can we sit down? Can we just talk? It's so nice here, it's warm and cozy. Do you hear that wind? Turgenev has that line, "...corner of the wind..." Right? It's nothing. Can I have some water?

PETER: I don't even know that line. I can't even say his name right.

ARKADINA: I haven't cried in so long. Last night, I went to see if the theater was still there.

PETER: I did hate you, I spit on your memory. I tore up your letters and photographs. But the whole time, I knew that I was yours forever. I don't have the strength to stop knowing you and I hate it. I can't stand it. I don't feel young anymore, I feel like I'm a million years old. And I have to keep learning everything.

ARKADINA: What are you talking about? Why are you talking like this? My horses are here, I have to go.

PETER: Where are you going?

ARKADINA: I don't know.

PETER: My uncle was really sick.

ARKADINA: Did you or did you not say that you would kiss the ground that I walk on? Come on. Fine. I'm so tired.

PETER: I just don't know why I'm doing anything or who I do it for, I'm serious.

ARKADINA: Yeah. I still love her. I love her more than I did before. Subject for a short story.

A moment.

Arkadina exits.

TREPLOV and TRIGORIN (PETER)

Treplov enters. He stands next to Trigorin as they both face forward.

TREPLOV: You make hearts beat at the same time every night, a flip of the page.

PETER: Yes, but I'd rather make my own heart beat quickly, so that I am the only one who can hear it.

TREPLOV: I want to know more of what you're talking about.

PETER and NINA

Nina enters.

NINA: Privet, Peter. Privet, Kostya. *[Hello, Peter. Hello, Kostya.]*

TREPLOV: *(Exiting.)* Privet... *[Hello...]*

PETER: Vera. *(Pause.)* I cannot deal with you as niece anymore.

NINA: But I'm not your niece. I am not your niece. In real life, I am not your niece. That's just in the play, idiot. Right? And why do you keep calling me Vera right now? My name is Nina. You're making me crazy. And I need to get ready. Do you love my hair?

PETER: Very. I am going to say it again. I can't stand you as a niece.

NINA: Ok. But I don't even play a niece in the play, actually! Now that I think about it. I'm not your niece in this piece. I don't understand what you're doing. I don't know how to say the right things or give you what – fuck it – I have no clue actually what you expect from me. As a friend or an actress. Or as a niece.

PETER: I know that. I was off-base. I mean. I don't know. I don't know. I don't have a niece in real life, or in the play. Obviously. I mean, I just wanted to know. I'd imagined all of these ways a person could be and two people could be together, that was different and real and safe. And about this structure, and I thought that I, well, with you, I could create it... But. It's like it never even happened. I never finished picturing how it could be. And I never, ever, not once, considered you. Can you believe that? You, who were to be the niece – what did you want or need? Is it a part for you?... I don't even know. So I/

NINA: Peter. *(She looks at her wrist.)* I have to go... *(Exiting.)*

PETER and ARKADINA (and POLINA)

Arkadina sits in the chair upstage of Peter. When she begins to speak, he goes and sits in the chair next to her.

ARKADINA: *(To Peter.)* I liked what you did in rehearsal today. It was strange and I didn't hear how it ended, but it left a very strong impression. You're very talented. You should keep at it.

Peter shakes Arkadina's hand vigorously, then hugs her impulsively. Arkadina pulls back slightly, their faces are very close, as if they might kiss.

ARKADINA: I don't mean for you to get all worked up. I don't think we have to be emotional about everything. Are you crying? What did I mean to say, I guess. Just that, it's clear you can work from a world of very high ideas. And that's awesome. Real works of art should be trying to get at those highest ideas. A real kind of beauty is pretty deep I think. *(Pause.)* You are so pale.

PETER: You think I should stick with it then?

ARKADINA: Yes. But try to make it very important.

PETER: You know. I've always lived my life really fully. I experienced everything I could, within certain confines – and not. And, I'm, sort of happy I think, in certain ways. But if I had the chance to feel what – like, what a certain kind of artist, certain kinds of people, must feel when they are making something and being themselves – then I imagine I could shed my own skin, my material being, and lift myself out of this world.

Polina enters.

POLINA: Where's Vera? I mean, Nina, whatever.

They don't answer. Polina stands there.

ARKADINA: *(To Peter.)* Your work has to have an absolutely clear, precise reason. You need to know why you're doing it, otherwise you end up getting too abstract and without goals, and you have to live with a kind of failure.

POLINA: *(To Arkadina and Peter.)* I need to say something to you. I want to say – I don't love my family, and I feel drawn to you. I feel so much closer to you. Help me. Help me, please, or I'll do something stupid. I'll ruin my life, I can't stand it anymore.

PETER: What? How can I help?

POLINA: I'm in so much pain. No one knows how much I'm suffering.

ARKADINA: You're all so highly strung. So highly strung. And such a lot of love.

Polina exits.

PETER: Rehearsal was weird today.

ARKADINA: I understood nothing, but I liked watching it. You acted with such sincerity. And the set was really nice.

Arkadina and Peter exit.

"PRIVET"

Polina, Masha, and Treplov sing "PRIVET."

Tak! Ya paloochil too rol'
Tak! Ya paloochil too rol'

S'yomka v Blefe Shaklova

Ty paloochil
Ty paloochil

Chtozh, zamechatel'no

Unas khvatit banok
Unas khvatit banok

Privet

YAKOV'S BUTT

Nina and Arkadina sit talking. Masha fixes her skateboard. Polina stands and smoke. They are talking amongst themselves initially in low Russian.

Treplov enters.

TREPLOV: So I found the pisspot... my nail clippers were with it. *(Pause.)* I mean. Weren't with it.

NINA: Brava.

MASHA: I hate the pisspot.

Masha exits.

ARKADINA: *(To Treplov.)* You're impossible.

POLINA: Where did you find the pisspot?

NINA: Can we please stop calling it the pisspot?

Peter rushes in.

PETER: So I got the part! Rehearsing in Yakov's butt, I mean bluff. We're rehearsing in Yakov's Bluff.

ARKADINA: You got it? Well, wonderful. You'll need to pack for town.

POLINA: *(To someone.)* Do we have enough jars?

NINA: Whoa. That's awesome. Amazing. When is it again?

Masha skateboards in to stage right of the group.

NINA: *(To Masha.)* Peter got cast in/

MASHA: In what?

NINA: "Stoli Nights." Is that even right? Peter. What is it called again?

PETER: Yeah, "Stoli Nights."

MASHA: *(To Peter.)* Ah! You got it. Easy come, easy go.

NINA: But, what about this show. When are you leaving again? Is it going to work to do both?

PETER: Yes, of course, I will make it work to do both.

NINA: Brava.

ARKADINA: Do you think this part is so good? Or does it pay really well?

MASHA: Oh, yes, Brava!

PETER: I can make it work to do both.

Pause.

POLINA: I am going to need your conflicts. This afternoon. Swift as a crane.

PETER: Well, they're not settled on that end, so, I have to let you know when I know mo/

POLINA: Well, we have a lot work to do on our end, so I'm going to need your conflicts fast as a flip toad. You have been committed and rehearsing this for over 37 weeks. It's not fair.

NINA: To us.

ARKADINA: I still smell that still, does anyone else…?

PETER: Okay. I understand. This may not work then. *(Pause.)* Do they have all the re-writes? I could learn some stuff now and/

POLINA: The script is not complete. So much is developed in the room, off your energy, you know. I don't know, I don't know/

NINA: Are you kidding me?? *(Exits.)*

Treplov enters, grabs Masha and kisses her. The others all turn and look. Masha takes Treplov by the arm and walks him offstage.

Polina exits.

PETER and ARKADINA

Peter and Arkadina move downstage.

PETER: Everything I hate is the opposite of right now. But then if fear is positive, then everything I hate is also here. Duh. If fear is positive, then I am not afraid of anything and that could be a really big problem. But then if I hate everything, including lists, then I will list out what I love.

ARKADINA: I do like women's breasts. But I'm not sure, maybe it's just the idea of them, and then it translates back to me and mine. And this is weird, I think, because it's not about actually touching them, in some way it is about mine being touched… but then it's about getting a peep too. But just looking can be so unsatisfying. I just don't know what I actually want, or, I'm not going to admit it, in a super real way.

PETER: Vera? To say that she is often in my thoughts… would be an understatement, for never a moment passes without my thinking of her! She is to my spirit what air is to physical existence! Everything is concentrated in her alone.

ARKADINA: Peter, I have never been able to make myself come by masturbating by myself. *(Pause.)* Okay. *(Small pause.)* And that is a kind of acting. I can't come unless someone is there, and even then they probably have to get involved. *(Pause.)* I hope you know. By now. That everything I hate. Is actually everything I love and am also afraid of. But also are probably the things I want to smother me, until I die. Now you get why I hate-slash-love everything.

MASHA DOES BENJAMIN BUTTON

POLINA: From the top of that section, please.

Everyone returns to center, except for Treplov who remains watching stage left.

They try to figure out who is sitting where.

TREPLOV: Does anyone need a chair?

Everyone ignores him.

POLINA: From the top of that section. Masha. *(Masha comes and stands next to Polina's chair.)* They want you to be very present. You don't have to rush your lines.

MASHA: I have no lines in this part.

POLINA: Okay, awesome. I need you to slow it down. As I said, be very present with the moment. Don't be acting it. Need real feelings, a real interest from you in the action. It can be beautiful. And weird. It just has to be... you know what they want. Slow exit, you're quite old. *(To all.)* Let's go.

Arkadina goes to Polina, whispers something in her ear, and returns to her seat.

Treplov has moved to the samovar upstage. After the sound of tea being poured from the samovar is heard, Treplov lifts in glass in salute, "Nastrovya."

Everyone ignores him.

The garden party rehearsal section begins:

PETER: I've always a soft spot for fishing.

POLINA: I'm sorry, can you start again?

PETER: I've always a soft spot for fishing.

NINA: I just can't imagine that just sitting around like that... is terribly creative.

ARKADINA: Oh, don't talk like that. Whenever somebody starts to talk about big ideas *(gesturing at Peter)*, just goes to pieces.

PETER: I remember in Moscow once/

OTHERS: Mos-CO/

ARKADINA: It's Mos-CO.

PETER: ...I remember in Mos-CO once, I saw a real old-timey dog-and-pony show. Glossiest coats I ever seen. Then we went to the opera and that famous bass Silva hit low C. We were sitting in the gallery at the time with the bass from our local choir. And imagine our surprise when all of a sudden we hear from him, "Brava, Silva!" A full octave lower! Like this. *(In a deep voice.)* "Brava, Silva!" *(Nina and Arkadina each repeat a version of "Brava, Silva." Pause.)* You could have heard a pin drop.

Long pause.

ARKADINA: *(Listening.)* Angels.

They all listen.

NINA: I must be going. Forgive me. *(Stands up, does a clumsy curtsy, and does not leave.)*

ARKADINA: It has to be time for lunch. *(Noticing Masha standing up very slowly.)* Is her leg asleep?

Peter, Arkadina, and Nina speak to each other about actorly concerns in Russian and English as Masha crosses slowly behind them holding her chair.

NINA: *(Noticing Masha.)* Oh my god, she didn't mean that slowly!

PETER: Gahh!

ARKADINA: Come on!

Treplov enters.

TREPLOV: Masha.

In Russian, Masha tells Treplov, "We meant to do better, but it came out as always." She exits.

PETER'S LIKE THE SUN

Treplov sizes up Peter who is also sort of Trigorin in this moment.

TREPLOV: Smart, simple, melancholy. I have your number.

PETER: Touché. But, you can't even grow a decent mustache. Can you?

TREPLOV: What do you think?

Peter moves to Treplov and touches his upper lip.

PETER: No.

TREPLOV: Fine. But I'm so sick of everyone thinking you and your hair – just cause it's a little brighter and less bristle-y than mine, that you and that cat smile, that you and your easy charm and smooth face, that you're like, you're like the sun! Whatever, you're not like sun. You are easy and big in your lightness, sure. But that is not just like the sun. It is a sneakily focused ambition that chooses exactly in its laconic moonshot who to lavish a ray on. Who to bumble-y make the one. Or not. But that's not the sun. That is you. And I make things. But what do you make? What do you really do that's so hard?

PETER: I know that I am of a value. I am expected to deliver within terms that ask that of me. So, yes, if you want some analogy, some sense of sun on the dacha roof, goddammit, here I am. *(Pause.)* But you have to figure out what that means for you. And then move on. Or you will go insane trying to not care and not figure it out. You'll be real paralyzed. And that's a waste. Cause you have something of yours. I'm taller. I have more horses. And your mother loves me. But love can be refracted. And you should know that.

NINA and POLINA

Nina has been sitting upstage next to Polina who stands. They watch as Peter crosses and exits. Nina looks up at Polina.

NINA: If you ever need my life, come and take it.

SPECIAL SKATEBOARD CROSS

Treplov crosses downstage front slowly pulling Masha who stands on her skateboard in a formal pose. After they cross completely to stage right, they stop and make a structured turn to move upstage at which point Nina joins the procession and holds Masha's other hand. A loud sound cue and music accompany this moment.

They have crossed to far upstage left when Arkadina enters from stage right and interrupts the moment.

TRIGORIN and ARKADINA

Arkadina faces Trigorin (Peter). The others watch briefly, then exit.

ARKADINA: All of you are in conspiracy to torture me today! *(She walks towards Trigorin.)* Have I gotten so old and disgusting that you dare to talk about other women to my face?

She walks and stands next to him. He pulls her towards him, she resists a bit, then they begin to kiss.

TRIGORIN: Anyone could walk in here.

ARKADINA: Let them, I'm not ashamed of my love for you. You're mine. *(Touching him.)* This is my forehead, these are my eyes, this beautiful, silken hair is all mine. You are all mine. You are so talented, so intelligent. You think this is just flattery? That I'm lying? Look into my eyes, look. Tell me I'm a liar. I'm the only one who knows what you're really worth. I'm the only one who ever tells you the whole truth. *(She steps away from him.)* Come with me? Will you? Don't leave me.

TRIGORIN: I have no will of my own. Never did. I always obey – is it possible that's attractive to women? Take me away, carry me off, but don't ever let me stray from your side.

ARKADINA: Whatever you want. Together then. *(Trigorin makes a note on his Blackberry.)* What are you writing?

TRIGORIN: I heard an awesome expression this morning, "virgin forests." It works.

Pause.

They exit in opposite directions..

MASHA and POLINA

Polina stands on stage alone smoking and looking out over the lake. Masha skates in looking up at birds flying above her. She sees Polina and comes to her.

MASHA: Half a V of geese – like one half – just flew over. *(Holds a gesture with one arm bent at the elbow.)*

POLINA: How many fish would you say are in the lake?

MASHA: Are you listening to me?

POLINA: Yes. I am listening.

MASHA: Do you want things you can't see?

Pause.

POLINA: No.

She passes her cigarette to Masha who takes a puff and passes it back.

MASHA: We (kind of) started doing stuff again – I mean – we did do stuff again. *(Pause.)* I'm really fucked up and I wanted it to happen.

POLINA: Okay.

MASHA: This is what it was like.

Masha kisses Polina the same way that Treplov kissed her.

POLINA: *(Pushing Masha off.)* Stop it! Stop it!

Masha walks away.

MASHA: See. This is how I am!

BIG RUSSIAN SCENE IN RUSSIAN

[The performers in the original production spoke a variety of phonetically learned Russian to accompany the actions and intentions of this scene. The dynamic of performers committing fully to the phonetics of a language they do not know and applying it improvisationally fuels the scene with a constant and precarious energy and magic as they move through what is described in the following italics.]

Nina passes by Masha saying hello and asking what her problem is. Masha snaps at her and exits.

Arkadina enters having an argument with Treplov, who has a white bandage wrapped around his head from an unacknowledged injury.

Nina pulls Arkadina aside to talk about a role she is working on. Arkadina listens and offers advice.

Peter walks in working on his lines. Arkadina sees Peter. Nina looks up, sees Peter, returns to her conversation with Arkadina. Peter watches them for a while, then goes back to work on his lines.

Masha comes backs in, adjusting part of her outfit or accessories. She sees Treplov by himself, goes to speak to him, and asks if she should wear a side ponytail for her audition. He is aggravated by this question and the whole scene in general after the squabble with his mother. He snaps at Masha.

Masha then goes and tries to talk to Nina. Nina sees her, but keeps talking to Arkadina, wanting time alone with her. Treplov walks over and says hi to Nina also. Nina gives a brief smile to Treplov, but keeps her focus on Arkadina, continuing to try to discuss acting with her. Masha tries again to talk to Nina. Treplov does too. Arkadina finally acknowledges Masha with a nod and greeting. Annoyed at losing Arkadina's attention, Nina suddenly snaps at all of them and walks away. Realizing she has made a scene, she stops and apologizes. Masha feels hurt and abandoned by Nina in this moment and yells "Davai!" ("Come on!") at her in an aggressive manner.

Everyone stops and looks at Masha. Peter sticks up for Nina, saying that she is doing the best she can and tells Masha to relax.

Masha tells Peter to mind his own business and walks over to Nina to try to speak with her directly. Treplov follows, trying to speak to Nina also.

Arkadina sees Treplov's ill-fated attempts to insert himself in the situation and starts to tell both Nina and Masha that Treplov is a good boy and they should pay attention to him. This sets off a nerve for Treplov, who finds it condescending and insincere.

He screams at his mother to leave him alone and then tries to rush offstage. He gets caught up in the curtains exacerbating his anger and humiliation as they twist around him. He finally frees himself from the curtains and storms back in. He screams at his mother and Peter that they are hacks. This makes Arkadina furious and she yells at Treplov, saying that he is a useless, unappreciative child who is also a bad artist.

Treplov is overcome. He sinks into the chair that is center stage.

Arkadina stands behind him, attempting to comfort him as the lights fades to a spotlight on mother and son.

The following is done in the English notated below.

TREPLOV: *(To Arkadina.)* People think I would give up everything to have success. I know they think that of me. And it's not true. I would give up everything I have, the smallest things I have clawed for, for you to have success. I swear to god.

ARKADINA: *(Continuing to hug and comfort Treplov.)* You're wrong. No one equates you with success. Not the way you carry on. We just bolster you. But you're nothing. You're not even Russian. Get away from me.

TREPLOV: You're cheap. In like three different ways.

ARKADINA: You're a failure. I've always thought that. But I've never said it out loud.

Treplov stands up and walks away, devastated.

[The performers return to speaking Russian to accompany the following actions and intentions.]

Masha goes to comfort Treplov as he walks away.

Arkadina reaches out and violently grabs Masha's arm to stop her: "Nyet!" ("No!").

Masha suddenly turns and walks to Peter asking if he will kiss her. They immediately begin to kiss. Everyone screams. In a state of shock, Nina whispers, "Masha!"

Peter says that he was just acting, but Polina finally bursts. She paces back and forth screaming at all of them in Russian (phonetically rendered below and followed by the English translation):

POLINA: Ostanovitess. Ostanovitess! Eta nee mozhet prodolzheet. Nyet. Nyet neekakova smissla. Yeslee vee ni hoteetye beet zdyess, yeslee eta ni delayet vass shastleevimee. Poyitee. Nyet neekakova smissla. Eta sleeshkom troodnah. Eta neekogdah nee boodet prekrass-nee. No, yeslee vee ni mozhetye vesstee poppeetkoo. Tolka poeedeetye. Lyooboy, vsye vee. Vertyeh menyeh, ya v ossnovnom nyenaveezhoo eta stolko, skolko vee dellayeteh. Nagrevahniye starovo chaya. Yedah malenkovo roolona sploheem masslom – Nye moy tsenahree metchtee… No ya tepper zdyess. Ee ya vereeyoo v vass. Ee v etom. Nesmotriya na vsyo dokazatelstvo obratnovo. Tepper ya ne neekakoi angell. No ya mog dazha oboeetiss byez massla. Ya peredanni… koi – chto. Horroshow. Noo? Noo?

[Stop. Stop!! This cannot continue. No. There is no point. If you do not want to be here, if this does not make you happy. Go. There is no point. This is too hard. It will never be perfect. But if you cannot commit to trying. Just go. Run along. Any, all of you. Believe me, I basically hate this as much as you do. Heating up old tea. Eating a small roll with bad butter – not my dream scenario either. But this is where I am now. And I do believe in you. And this. Despite all the evidence to the contrary. Now I'm no angel. But I could even do without butter. I am committed … to … something. Okay. (She looks around at all of them.) Well? Well?]

Pause.

Everyone has quieted in shame during Polina's monologue. As they exit, Arkadina assures Polina that they will be prepared to rehearse.

Masha mutters that she was just acting too.

Polina sits center and speaks in English.

POLINA: We were happy before, remember? We were. Everything was clear and warm and a kind of happiness. Remember? People and lions, and eagles and partridges.

The horned deer, the geese, and the spiders. Silent fishes dwelling silently in the sea. Starfish and every unseen star in the sky turning around and around – all have been extinguished. The sorrowful moon vainly lights her pale lamp. The meadows no longer stir to the cry of the cranes, and the hum of the June bugs is silent in the linden grove.

"SLAVSA RUS"

Led by Masha, everyone re-enters to sing in Russian along to the track of "Slavsa Rus" by Arkona. Polina accompanies on guitar.

MASHA

Oi-da, matushka
Nochka-Svarogovna
Skroi sedye zavety ottsov
Ot glaza chernogo liuta voroga
V gushe sviaschennyh lesov

EVERYONE

Snova, serdtsem zamiraia
Slovo molvim, chut' dysha
Slav'sia, Matushka rodnaia!
Slav'sia, Russkaia dusha!

Gherez debri vekovye
Skvoz' dalekie kraia
Molvim, bratiia rodnye
Slav'sia, Rus', Zemlia moia!

When they song ends all exit except for Masha and Nina.

MASHA and NINA

Masha and Nina each carry a chair downstage center and sit down facing each other at an angle. They each put their hair up in a high bun. Nina takes off her headband and hands it to Masha.

MASHA: This is what it feels like, knowing that someone (is there), not there anymore. It's like, I can see half of my heart and it's out and it is walking around and it's pale pink. And it is really big *(she gestures with her hands)*, and not that my heart is so big – but that half that I could see, that was out and walking around, it had legs and it was really big, it was life-size, it was walking, and it was just one half, and it was very pale pink, and I could feel like I was wanting to reach for it and I was reaching for it, but as it was walking, while this was happening, it was being erased. By like a giant eraser. So it was like this half of my heart was out there walking and I could see it, but it was being erased and I was reaching and reaching and it was disappearing. That whole half of my heart.

Nina cries. Then Masha cries. They have to make each other cry.

And it would be easier if it was just gone. But watching it fade.

NINA: You will probably always have someone who loves you.

MASHA: But not like that.

Masha exits.

NINA and TREPLOV

Nina is there. Treplov comes in.

TREPLOV: Your eyes look a little like they were crying... that's not good.

NINA: It's just... I'm still catching my breath. I have to leave in a half an hour – I lost my other cell phone – we'd better hurry. You mustn't keep me any later, for God's sake. My father doesn't know I'm here.

TREPLOV: Actually it's time to begin, we should call the others.

NINA: My father and his wife won't let me come here. They say you're all a bunch of bohemians. They're afraid I really will become an actress. But. My heart is full of you.

TREPLOV: *(Going to Nina.)* Are we alone?

They stand close, Treplov behind Nina.

NINA: What kind of tree is that?

TREPLEV: It's elm. *(Pause. He steps away.)* I'm going to kill myself pretty soon.

NINA: I don't know you.

TREPLEV: After I stopped knowing you. You've changed toward me, you look at me with a cold stare, I just embarrass you, my very existence embarrasses you. Admit it.

NINA: You're so crazy lately. Everything you say is some kind of strange symbol. Like this text message. I don't understand it. Sorry. I'm just too stupid to understand you.

TREPLEV: It started when my play fell apart in the fall. Women don't forget failure, I know it. And I burned it all, every page. You just cannot understand how unhappy I am. You can't, you've become so cold to me, it's so weird and strange. Like I woke up to find the lake was gone or drained into the earth. You just said that you're too stupid to understand me. What is there to understand?! No one liked my play, you hate how I think artistically, you can't imagine kissing me. I know. I know it! There's a little worm in my brain, damn him along with my pride, he keeps sucking my blood, sucking, like a creepy little snake.

NINA: I would like to continue with this rehearsal. I'm trying really hard to think about things that are positive and keep it together. I think you'll realize later that it's you who doesn't understand me. Okay. And I feel just as ruined as you.

Treplev looks at her. She looks back.

TREPLEV: It's not even sunny out and all of a sudden, I can hear it, you're like, shining. *(Pause.)* I am out of here.

Treplov turns stage right and starts to exit upstage. Nina circles upstage too. Treplov runs after Nina and pulls her arm, so that it surprises and hurts her for real. They physically fight against each other for a moment. Then stop and pull away.

NINA: I am always, always thinking of you. And I really hate you. *(Pause.)* I mean, not that.

Nina exits.

MASHA DOES HER AUDITION

Masha enters. Treplov hands her a script for her audition.

MASHA: I don't need it. (*She takes off her fur hat. The other actors watch from stage left.)*

The daughter of an insurance person, a former hotel student… raised on respect for who had what, kissing the rabbi's hands, worshipping the ideas of others, and giving thanks for every stuffed animal, receiving frequent punishment, making the rounds as a camp counselor without the right shoes, fighting, chasing cats, enjoying dinners at the homes of wealthy relatives, needlessly hypocritical before God and older people merely to acknowledge her own insignificance… I squeeze that loser out of myself drop by drop and on waking one hot morning, find that the blood coursing through my veins is no longer the blood from before, but that of a real human being.

Masha bows her head and moves upstage.

ARKADINA

Arkadina stands speaking to herself and to Nina. Polina stands nearby.

ARKADINA: This one role. I didn't even speak… I know so much about these people. It's crazy. It's a way of staying in some part of something. *(Pause.)* I remember so much stuff. It washes over me and takes away my breath. The memories creep and ease in, unapproachable and intimate.

NINA: I don't know.

ARKADINA: This assault of unassailable meaning and memory… it buckles me. Completely to my knees. I want to watch it. But I am in it.

TREPLOV: *(Entering.)* Mum. I found your watch. It wasn't under the rugs…

Peter has entered stage left. Arkadina crosses the stage and moves to him. Still within herself, she holds his arm and looks out towards the audience.

ARKADINA: I just want to feel something – and I want to feel it when I am up here. But it's like, I can't even feel it still *(she raises her arms)* or I don't know how *(she slowly lowers her arms)* or… "I remember laughter, noise, gunshots, and romance, romance…."

She turns upstage and is met by Treplov. All now remain in various parts of the stage. Peter and Nina step to the foreground.

PETER and NINA

NINA: *(To Peter.)* Can I see your skateboard?

Peter puts his skateboard down and with a slight push of his foot, sends it towards towards Nina. Nina places the stuffed seal she is holding on the skateboard and gently pushes it forward.

NINA: Peter, look. Have you ever seen anything so cute? Ever? He's from the lake. And he brings me luck.

PETER: Nina. It is sort of beautiful. I would never have known of that. I don't have good luck tokens. I am a male actor in that way. Just me, my beard. And all the right cadences. But you. Look at you – you have the lake and that seal and your hair – it is. It is quite beautiful.

NINA: Peter, I've lost my voice. I'm really freaked out for this show.

Peter goes to Nina.

PETER: No. My baby beet, my niece. You have everything it takes. You will say everything that was rehearsed. You will pause at just the right times. You will make that eye contact with the audience that melts knees. You will find Trigorin and stab him in the heart. You will trail one hand against that scenic tree. Pathos will trickle. For the part where you spread your arms out and fly, they will lift you more quietly than you have ever been lifted.

NINA: What about you Peter? Did you have a good summer?

PETER: Ah, shit. Who even knows. But listen. You are going to kill it tonight. Your voice will rise up so strong and beautiful that questions of pride and shame and work and false meaning will definitively fall away. Your voice will rise up so strong that by the end of Act II, we will question if we need Act III, but we will die if we don't get it. You will probably lose your voice in the middle of Act III, but when you return as a teenage mother performing pantomime on a train, you will have the best dress ever sewn. *(Pause.)* Yes. That is what will happen.

NINA: Yes. Oh god.

PETER: It's okay.

NINA: Yes, here I am. This is me then. The shore of a lake, a young girl who's spent her whole life beside it. A girl like me. I love the lake the way a seagull does.

PETER: Yes. You are the seagull. You are the brightest bird. You are the niece. In all of my dreams. You have given me that. Your talent is so big.

Polina beckons Peter over to stage left.

Nina stays center delivering her text.

NINA: Yes. I'm the seagull. *(Pause.)* No, that's not it. *(Pause.)* I'm an actress. That's it. That's totally it. I am an actress and the seagull.

Treplov walks towards Nina.

TREPLOV: Let me look at you. It's warm here. *(He stands beside her.)* This used to be a sitting room.

Do I look different?

Masha walks forward, holding her skateboard, spinning one wheel, as she counts backwards, "dych sit, dyeh-vit, voh-syem, syem, shest, pyat, che-ti-ryeh, tree, dvah, ah-deen..." ("10, 9, 8, 7, 6, 5, 4, 3, 2, 1...").

All six performers line the very downstage edge of the stage facing the audience. They are lit very brightly. The music rises to its height.

Masha screams "Knenyetz!" ("End!").

Blackout.

End of play

Privet

from Half Straddle's Seagull (Thinking of you)

Music by Chris Giarmo

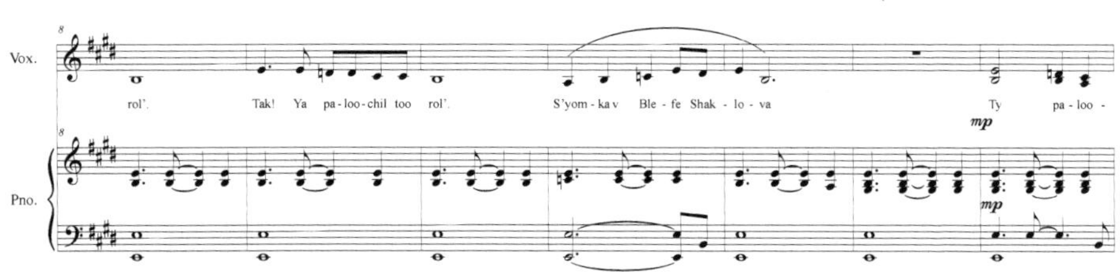

ARKADINA
аркадина
Benefit Boi-ing concealer #2
MAC eyeshadow in Honey Lust
Nars Orgasm Blush
Diorshow black Mascara
MAC Eye Kohl in Smolder
Products used:
MAC lip penzil in cherry
Rimmel lipstick - Kate Moss Red
• Benefit Boi-ing concealer #2
• MAC Eyeshadow in Honey Lust
• Diorshow Black Mascara
• MAC Eye Kohl in Smolder
• MAC Lip penzil in Cherry
• Rimmel lipstick in Kate Moss Red
• Nars Orgasm Blush

MASHA

Маша

Products used:
• Benefit Boing concealer #1
• Benefit High Beam
• Nars Orgasm blush
• MAC eyeshadow in gesso
• MAC brow pencil in Lingering
• Clinique gold eyeliner
• MAC lip pencil in Nightmoth
• Diorshow black mascara
• MAC lipstick in Cyber
MAC brow pencil in Lingering
Diorshow Black Mascara
MAC eyeshadow in GESSO
Clinique Gold eyeliner
Benefit High Beam
Nars Orgasm blush
Benefit Boing #1
MAC Lipliner in Nightmoth
MAC lipstick in Cyber

NINA
НИНА
Diorshow mascara in BLACK
MAC Eye Kohl in Fascination
MAC brow pencil in Brunette
MAC eye kohl in Costa Riche
Benefit High Beam
MAC blush in Dollymix
Benefit blush in Dandelion
MAC lipliner in whirl
Revlon lipstick in Persian Melon
Benefit Boing concealer #1
Products Used
· Diorshow mascara Black
· MAC Eye Kohl in Fascination
· MAC Brunette brow pencil
· MAC Costa Riche eye kohl
· Benefit High Beam
· MAC blush in Dollymix
· Benefit Boing Concealer #1
· Benefit Blush in Dandelion
· MAC lipliner in Whirl
· Revlon lipstick in Persian Melon

POLINA

ПОЛИНА

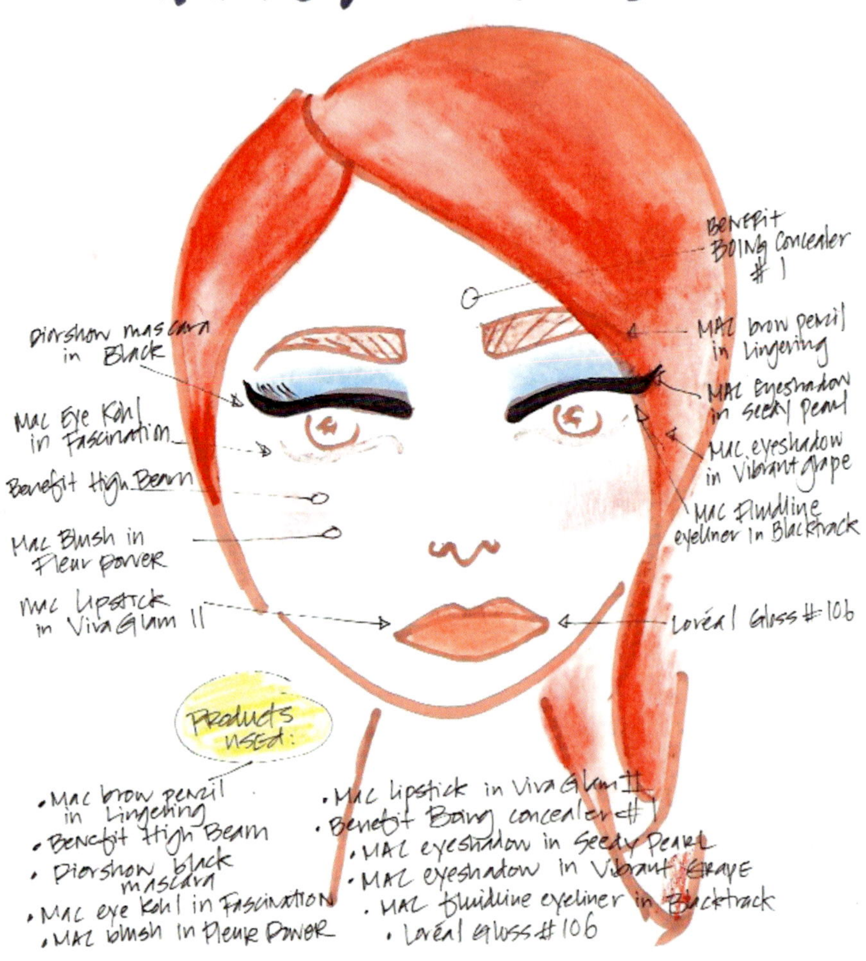

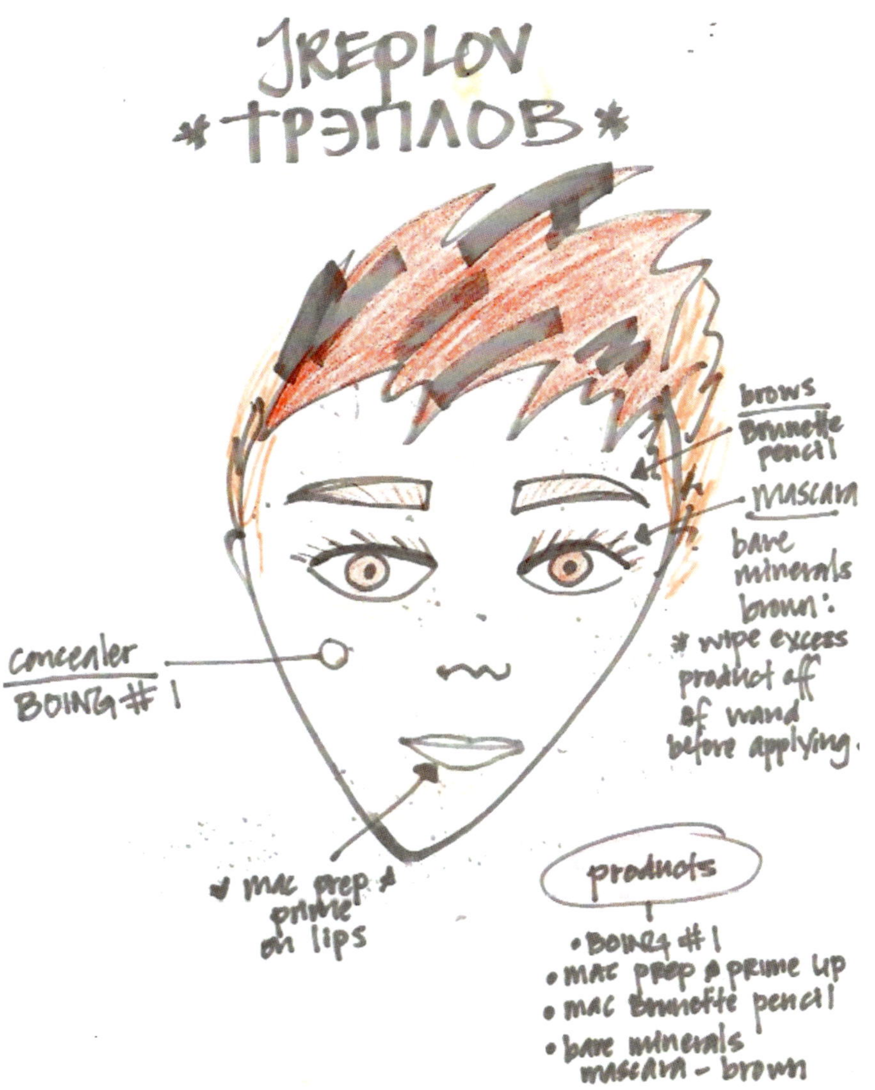
JREPLOV
ТРЭПЛОВ
brows
Brunette pencil
mascara
bare minerals brown:
* wipe excess product off of wand before applying.
concealer
BOING #1
* mac prep & prime on lips
products
• BOING #1
• mac prep & prime lip
• mac Brunette pencil
• bare minerals mascara - brown

PETER

Петер

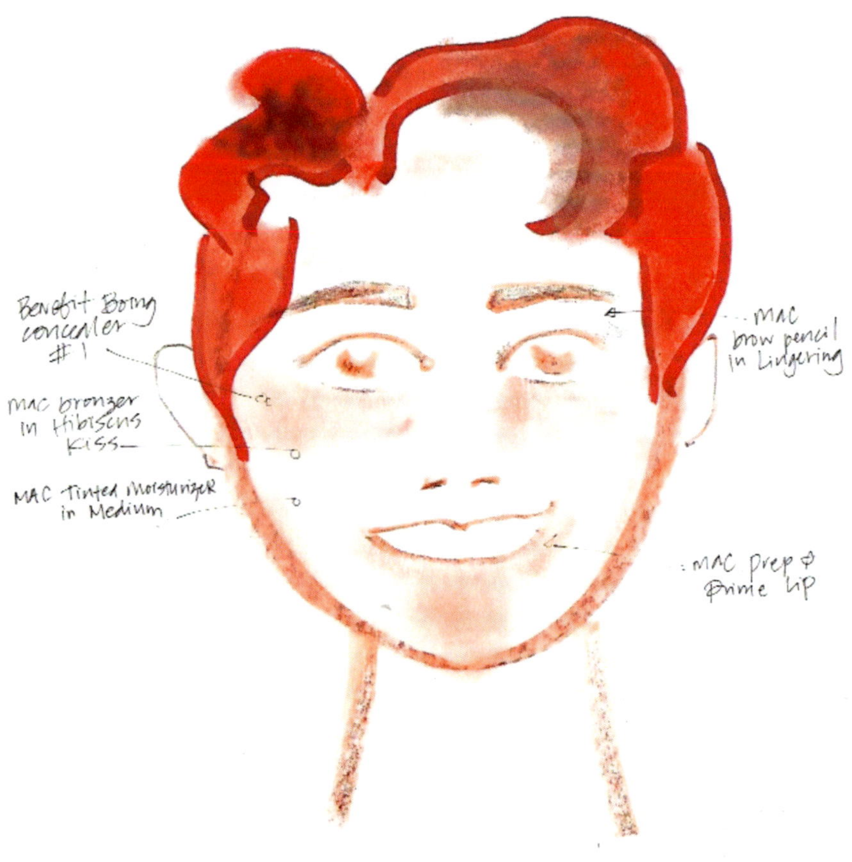
Benefit Boing concealer #1
MAC bronzer in Hibiscus Kiss
MAC Tinted Moisturizer in Medium
MAC brow pencil in Lingering
MAC Prep & Prime Lip

Away Uniform

Characters and Setting

Farah and **Jem**, girls that look like they could be anywhere from 17 to 19 years old.

Jayjay, a man that could be anywhere from early 30s to late 40s, effeminate and not-effeminate, depending. Wears a t-shirt with the sleeves cut off or a denim vest, jeans or sport shorts, and white sneakers with horsehair on them.

They are on the Plains. It is simple, vast, small, and beautiful.

Addressing the Athletics of this Play

In certain important ways, this is a sports play. Farah and Jem do field hockey drills in several parts of the play, and the athleticism of those moments should be thoughtfully attended to so that the actions – passing, dribbling, and stickwork – look like the awkwardly natural second nature of teenage girls who had played the sport for at least several years.* Also, proper field hockey sticks and balls should be used.

When Jayjay briefly does some stickwork, he should be attempting the correct form, but it does not have to be quite as natural as it is for the girls.

*The author is happy, if asked, to provide further information on the correct ways to practice the field hockey passing, dribbling, stickwork called for (and the "Inside/Outside" warm-up that Jayjay does).

SCENE 1

Jem and Farah walk into the space. Farah has a field hockey stick and does stickwork with a ball as she walks forward. She lies down. Jem sits against her and looks out. She tilts her head to one side. She sits for like 30 seconds. She stands up and looks out more. Then she goes and sits on the small braided rug stage right and picks up her field hockey stick.

JEM: I just never got back on the bus.

FARAH: *(Still lying down, but waking up.)* Okay.

JEM: I didn't. We won the game. I was still in my uniform and I was just like/

FARAH: Fuck it!

JEM: Exactly! I was like fuck it!

Jem goes over and sits on Farah holding her down.

JEM: What was I like?

FARAH: You were like fuck it.

JEM: What?

FARAH: Fuck it. You pulled your underwear off, but left your uniform on and just like ran and hid behind that dumpster.

JEM: Oh my god. I can't believe I did that! What number was I?

FARAH: I'm so tired still.

JEM: Tell me what number I was.

FARAH: You were a halfback the year before and defense had higher numbers.

JEM: Yeah. What number was I?

FARAH: 19. We were both number 19.

JEM: But on different teams, dipshit.

FARAH: *(Suddenly sits up.)* I know, but like, holy shit. How weird that we were the same number?

JEM: It's like a really lucky number right.

FARAH: It's like the luckiest number ever.

SCENE 2

Farah and Jem pass a field hockey ball back and forth with field hockey sticks.

FARAH: Let's do the one that starts at the beginning.

They continue passing the field hockey ball back and forth.

FARAH: Let's do that one that starts at the beginning.

JEM: Okay. I can do that.

Farah passes the ball to Jem and they stop passing back and forth. Jem puts her hand up to her ear to be a telephone.

JEM: *(To Farah.)* Make a ring sound.

FARAH: Br-iii-nnng.

JEM: *(Into the fake phone.)* Oh, hello. *(Pause.)* Ooooh. Honey. *(Pause.)* You sound mad busy. Busy like a bumble bee. *(Pause.)* Okay, okay, I call you later. Shit man. That ain't cool.

She looks at Farah. Then passes the ball to her.

JEM: Br-iing/

FARAH: Can the ring be louder/

JEM: Br-iii-nnng.

FARAH: *(Farah answers her fake hand phone. Long pause.)* Awww, homes. Why you gotta play like that? You know, I ain't got nothin' left to give. My kicks are supa beat. And my beats are like sooooo dry. Hey baby. Blow me up later?

JEM: Ughh, that's fucking retarded. Do it again. Br-iing.

FARAH: *(Farah answers her fake hand phone.)* Aww, homes. You know I don't wanna play like that. You all fly and shit. And I just wanna rock it like you know I can. And, oooh, my beats are soooooo dry. But also like… wetter? *(She stands up.)* Oh my god, I hate this. This is just. I can't do it now/

JEM: No, that was really good. Do it again. That's like last time. It was good. Just do it. The crawling's real good.

FARAH: I know it is.

Farah gets on her knees, mimes holding a phone to her ear, and crawls slowly back towards Jem.

FARAH: Hey.

JEM: *(Into her mimed phone.)* Hey.

FARAH: So. You wanna come over later?

JEM: Yeah, I might.

FARAH: Oh, ok. Do you have a sleeping bag?

JEM: Come on… what?

FARAH: Come on… baaa-by. Do you have a sleeping bag?

JEM: Try.

FARAH: Come on, baby. *(Pause.)* You wanna come over. *(Pause.)* Like later. Do you have a sleeping bag?

Pause.

JEM: That's pretty good. I think you should do it without the sleeping bag part though. *(Pause.)* I'm super tired.

FARAH: But now I'm into it. One more. Please. I want to do the other one.

JEM: Later. I'm gonna go see if there's anything to eat.

FARAH: There's one thousand years of okra. Will you get me some too?

Jem exits.

SCENE 3

Farah sits kneeling. She starts to move in like a trance-ish like dance, real slowly and then starts to stand up. Weird, blown-out music starts to play underneath as she steps forward in her slow, strange dance. The beat drops into it. Jem dances into the room in her own strange way. They dance like animals who live underground who don't know that music is supposed to make you dance. They fall down sometimes and there is an almost shameful ecstasy that comes into their dancing every so often. They don't interact with each other as they dance.

Jayjay enters and watches for a little bit.

JAYJAY: CUT IT OUT, maybe.

Farah stops, but Jem keeps dancing as the music begins to fade in volume.

JEM: What are you gonna do?

JAYJAY: Crap off.

FARAH: Jayjay.

JEM: Farah. *(Pause.)* What are you gonna do Jayjay?

JAYJAY: I said, crap off.

Farah stops dancing, Jem continues in the silence.

JEM: These are my moves.

FARAH: Yeah. Good ones.

JAYJAY: Fuck. I'm tired.

FARAH: Jayjay, do you wanna bench?

Farah gets down on her hands and knees.

JAYJAY: No. I don't want a goddamned bench.

FARAH: Here, I'll make you a bench.

Jem slowly stops dancing as she looks at Farah on her knees and lifts her gaze to stare at Jayjay.

JEM: *(Walking right up to Jayjay.)* Fuck off.

Jayjay and Jem are face to face, as he slowly scratches his ass with a creepy up and down claw gesture.

JAYJAY: Oh for fuck's sake, relax.

Jayjay looks at Jem as he circles her and starts to exit. He looks back and leaves.

Jem puts her hand in Farah's hair and pulls her into a standing position.

JEM: Cut it out.

FARAH: You.

SCENE 4

Jayjay is in some kind of athletic warm-up trance. He snaps his fingers and shifts his shoulders from side to side. He plays a bit with a field hockey ball and a stick.

Farah is off to one side, painting a fingernail, not paying attention.

JAYJAY: Four more, three more, two more, and take it to the right…

Oh yeah, that's it. That's the shit. That warm-up shit. What are those little peacocks always doing? It's–

Oh yeah… *(Starts to do an"Inside / Outside" warm-up, lifting his feet to his hands.)*

Inside, outside, outside, in – ahhh… fuck! My ass. My goddamn ass muscle – fuck. *(To God.)* I know what you're up to asshole. *(Kind of towards Farah.)* Shitheads, warm up that corn pad. Elvis needs a rub.

Jayjay passes Jem as he exits.

JEM: You're not supposed to use the round side of the stick, Jayjay.

SCENE 5

Farah is standing up with her arms above her head and her palms out wide. Jem kneels down in front of her.

Farah speaks kind of like preaching.

FARAH: The struggle will be hard.

Jem speaks kind of like she is testifying.

JEM: Uh-huh.

FARAH: I SAID, the struggle will be hard. Oh yes. The road will be long. The water will be high/

JEM: Oh, yeah.

FARAH: The road will be long. The water will be high. The struggle will be hard. Oh, so hard. The struggle will be hard/

JEM: Say it.

FARAH: The struggle will be hard, but not sad.

JEM: Oh no.

FARAH: Oh no. Oh no. No no no. The struggle will be hard, but not sad.

JEM: Mmmm-hmmm.

FARAH: The struggle will be joyous.

JEM: Oh yes, oh, yes.

FARAH: Out from the garden, out in the weeds. This goodness/

JEM: Oh yes.

FARAH: Our goodness will grow.

JEM: Amen.

FARAH: Like the biggest pumpkin. It is growing. *(Pause.)* I feel it now. Oh, I feel it. *(Starts to shake and tremble.)* It's here. *(Her hands reach in front of her.)* Oh, it's here. It's here. Our goodness. This goodness. It's hard and real.

And it's here in the cabinets, and the tools, and it is in the garden.

JEM: That green, green garden. Turn it brown.

FARAH: *(Still trembling.)* That green, green garden.

Farah slowly starts to fall backwards. Jem catches her from behind in a slow hug.

FARAH: Oh shit.

Pause.

JEM: Yeah. *(Pause.)* That was pretty good.

FARAH: Really?

JEM: Yeah. You're good.

FARAH: Oh my god. It was kind of intense.

Pause.

JEM: I don't know about the pumpkin.

FARAH: What? No. I felt that. I felt it. That's what was like, the thing that was growing. I feel like that works.

JEM: Alright.

Pause.

FARAH: I'm serious.

Longer pause.

JEM: Farah. *(Pause.)* Farah.

FARAH: What? *(Long pause.)* Yeah.

JEM: Nothing.

FARAH: Just say it.

Pause.

JEM: Nothing.

FARAH: Shut up.

JEM: So, is that everything?

FARAH: Yeah, it's all I've got right now.

Pause.

JEM: Yeah. You're pretty good.

FARAH: Thank you.

MY BABY INTERLUDE

Farah puts on her fuzzy leopard-print coat and crosses the stage snapping. Jem puts on her field hockey pullover and blows a whistle. Farah snaps them into a slow, dazed torch version of the song "Morning Train (Nine to Five)." They sing together, unaccompanied, doing synchronized choreography.

My baby takes the morning train
He works from nine till five and then

He takes another home again
To find me waitin' for him

Anything I want
Only when he's with me
I catch a light
Only when he gives me
Makes me feel alright

My baby takes the morning train
He works from nine till five and then
He takes another home again/

SCENE 6

The girls are finishing the song interlude when there is a thumping sound offstage. They pause.

JEM: Goddammit. That fucking skinny ass fucker is home.

FARAH: God!

JEM: Why's he here now?

FARAH: Storm's brewing? Or he wants that fertilizer so he can make that bullshit he snorts. *(She walks upstage and peers out.)* He's gone. He's walking towards the barn.

JEM: Once I saw him snort that fertilizer shit with his ass.

FARAH: Cut it out.

JEM: No, I'm totally serious.

FARAH: But he has like the flattest ass ever.

JEM: I know. That's what was amazing. The clouds were a'brewing. The sky was so goddamn dark. And he was wearing these sport shorts.

FARAH: Where the fuck would he get those?

JEM: I don't know. And he just pulled them right down.

FARAH: Did you see his?

JEM: Yes. Thank you.

FARAH: Sickness!

JEM: I know. Anyways, he didn't have any underwear on cause those sick little shorts had built-in shit and they are at his knees and he tries to squat down and put his ass right above the pile of stuff.

FARAH: What!? Oh my god. Shut up. What stuff? What stuff? What are you talking about? Oh my god. I can't stand it. I'm freaking out!

JEM: That shit!! I told you, I saw him try to snort that fertilizer crap up his ass.

FARAH: Oh my god. Okay.

JEM: But when his shorts were at his knees he couldn't get his butt low enough and he got stuck like halfway down there and he would try to like dip his butt down to reach it, but there was no way when he was doing that, that he could also try to suction stuff up with his asshole.

FARAH: Is this real?

JEM: Yes. I was dying.

FARAH: Where was I?

JEM: Out in the field or the barn or something. I wanted to tell you about it so badly.

FARAH: This is fucking amazing.

She walks over and puts one hand on Jem's shoulder.

JEM: Yeah, I know. Then he realized he had to push those shorts all the way down and he did that and they were at his ankles so then he could actually get his asshole practically all the way to the floor. And he tried to suction like that.

FARAH: Oh shit. No! What. What happened? Cut it out.

JEM: Yeah. It was like he was kind of pushing it around the floor, like some of the fertilizer may have gone up there by mistake, but it wasn't like sucked up.

FARAH: Oh shit. I'm dying. Shut up. Did he ever see you?

JEM: He got really pissed off. And pulled those shorts up.

FARAH: When did I come back?

JEM: Like, right after.

FARAH: So, it's kinda like I saved you.

JEM: Whatever. That fucker didn't.

Jayjay does a slow Canadian Cross.

JAYJAY: Watch the F-bombs, baby rats.

SCENE 7

Jem is braiding Farah's hair.

Jayjay enters humming part of "American Music" by the Violent Femmes... "Every time I look at that ugly moon, it reminds me of you, it reminds me of you uh-oh, uh-oh, uh-oh..." He squats down near the girls.

FARAH: What?

JEM: What? Jayjay.

JAYJAY: *(Singing.)* "It reminds me of you – uh-oh, uh-oh, uh-oh!" *(Stops singing.)* Got any wheat germ? Seriously, duders, I'm starving. And I feel like I have an infection.

FARAH: Ugh. You're so sick.

JAYJAY: SHUT THE FUCK UP.

JEM: You shut the fuck up.

JAYJAY: You don't want to do that.

JEM: Maybe I do? *(Crawls quickly towards him.)*

FARAH: *(To Jem.)* Cut it out.

JAYJAY: Don't even, you little butthole.

FARAH: Yeah. Please don't be a butthole, Jem.

JAYJAY: *(To Farah.)* I can't even go there right now. So shut your pusshole and leave it alone.

Jayjay has his hand on Jem's head to stop her crawl. He kneels down in front of her, keeping his hand on her head. He picks his nose and slowly lifts up a giant booger on his finger. He holds the booger in front of Jem's face.

FARAH: You are so disgusting.

JAYJAY: *(Still holding the booger in front of Jem's face, but looking at Farah.)* Whatever. *(Pause.)* I make so much more money than you.

FARAH: Jayjay, I don't even have any money. I don't have a job. I mean, you drive anyways. You have a job. I don't even drive.

JAYJAY: Fuck yeah, I do.

JEM: Fixing pneumatic blasting is not anything. It's total bullshit.

Jem licks the booger off of his finger and stands up.

JEM: Jesus christ, Jayjay, get a fucking life.

FARAH: Yeah. Beat it.

JAYJAY: Oh. I might.

Pause.

Jayjay stands in front of Farah. She doesn't flinch.

Pause.

JAYJAY: I'll make pancakes.

Farah looks at Jem.

FARAH: Well. I'll eat them.

JEM: And, if it's not too much of a bother, can you use milk that's from an actual animal and not from whatever human you managed to test out on that stupid contraption?

JAYJAY: I'm all out of that shit anyways. *(Walking to exit.)* My ass itches.

JEM: Dude.

SCENE 8

Jem and Farah take in the Plains around them. They stand and look out. It is a moment when evening is setting.

Jayjay enters with his fluorescent-bulbed farm implement. He does some farm work with the implement and then resumes singing the lyrics to "American Music."

I need a date to the prom
Would you like to come along
But nobody would go to the prom with me baby

You were born too late
I was born too soon
Every time I look at that ugly moon

It reminds me of you
It reminds me of you

You were born too soon
I was born too late
Every time I look at that ugly lake
It reminds me of me
It reminds me of me

Uh-oh uh-oh uh-oh

SCENE 9

Jem and Farah do close-up passbacks for a while with their field hockey sticks and the ball.

FARAH: That one episode, let's do that one, remember that one? Please.

Farah stops playing. Jem continues to do stickwork by herself.

JEM: Fuck that, dude. I don't remember any episode.

FARAH: Come on. It's the one you wrote on the side of the playhouse.

JEM: I probably wrote it in blood, Farah. Which means it's licked off by now. Dipshit.

FARAH: Holy fucking shit! You're the dipshit/

JEM: I love you. *(Pause.)* I can't do that episode right now. I'm tired. *(Looking directly at Farah.)* I just want a story. Or something.

Farah stands up.

FARAH: Which one?

JEM: Me coming here. That one, please.

FARAH: Okay. *(Pause.)* I just, wait, how many goals had you scored that season?

JEM: Well, that's the thing. Not that many. I played midfield a lot of the time then, which meant I played back and up. But tell me about the one game and then what happened next.

Jem paces back and forth slowly and fast with her stick as Farah speaks.

FARAH: Okay, at that one game. It was like really sunny. And the bus ride there was so yellow. And the sky. That sky was so, so blue. And you rode over that road. And it was warm. Not hot. It was like four o'clock. And you had taped up your one shinguard. And you had a ponytail that was already sweaty, and/

JEM: Oh, yeah.

FARAH: And remember, right before the game, you couldn't find your mouthguard/

JEM: Uh-huh.

FARAH: And, you felt. You felt very confident that day. You existed on your own. You were very good that season.

JEM: I was fit as a fucking fiddle.

FARAH: You were. That's the thing. You were in, like the zone. You knew then that there could be an actual, real zone. And that you were in it. That your muscles and their patterns were real. That toughness could be learned and then forgotten so it was just like there. And that you could step onto the grass with your cleats and know all the steps for each thing that would come at you that you could never plan for. And that you could laugh. And do like high-fives and feel strong and separate in that feeling. And that when they asked you to play up. Go up. Go up. Remember, isn't that what they said?

JEM: Yeah, yeah.

FARAH: And right, then, you were even kind of nervous. Which was perfect actually. And the sun was like religious and you could move your arms in all the right ways. And you could run backwards and sideways and be in all the right spots. And there was everyone there. And it was just like practice. How did that happen? And when the moment came you stepped forward and it was, you scored. You scored. Remember, the first goal. Remember, Jem?

JEM: I feel like I overreacted and jumped really high or something.

FARAH: Maybe. But it was still warm. And then you scored again. And a third time. Holy shit! Oh my god!

JEM: I know. Oh my god. And then I just walked off to the side.

FARAH: And by then it was dark.

JEM: And I pulled my underwear right down and just off. And I hid.

FARAH: And I was here.

JEM: Yeah.

JEM: All the way in the Plains.

FARAH: *(She touches Jem's head.)* Yes, the fucking Plains.

SCENE 10

They are all there. Jem is doing stickwork. Jayjay makes a headband on Farah's head with her hair.

JAYJAY: *(To Farah.)* Put your leg out.

FARAH: Why?

JAYJAY: Put it out.

Farah puts her leg out. Jayjay pushes up her jeans and breathes in the bottom part of her leg.

JAYJAY: That's it, those. Those pale, palest dusty leg hairs. That's what I like.

FARAH: Why?

JEM: Shut up, Farah.

FARAH: No, why?

JAYJAY: They remind me of God.

JEM: You're such a bullshitter.

JAYJAY: No, I ain't, girlfriend. Shut your piehole.

FARAH: Jayjay/

JAYJAY: What? I am as usual. Just doing God's work. This is a farm.

JEM: You think he even knows where you are? Let alone has his cockles attuned to your fucking needs. He doesn't listen to you Jayjay. No way. He doesn't even know where we are. No one can hear us.

JAYJAY: SHUT IT. Goddamn right, he listens.

Farah moves downstage and sits in a sermon position, listening. She beckons Jem to join her.

JAYJAY: First of all, I'm pretty sure he knows I give a fuck-all about his stupid-ass son. *(To God.)* Right? Hey God, hey – I ask, on this glorious day of the Lord *(He mimes a bleeding, pissing Jesus on the cross.)* Fuck that! Right. *(He raises his middle finger up.)* That you let me worship in my way and not bug me.

See, he listens. He has to. He gave me this fucking body, and these pains, and these oddnesses, and all. So. He has to. *(Pause.)* And what I'm saying, what I say when the dust rises and the walls of this house creak, he hears. *(To God.)* I know it's you. And I know you know that. *(Pause.)* When my scars burn, and my ankles turn in. When you gave me this body, God, you wanted to remind me. But here's the thing. I exist outside any system/

FARAH: Jayjay. Hey.

Jayjay holds up his finger to silence her.

JAYJAY: Yet. Yet. Yet, I am now tasked with these systems you have asked me to make. And I'm doing alright. I am doin' alright. I know it is your work that we do. A working farm here. And God, you are the chafe and the peas. You are in my contraption. And I will fucking make you proud.

JEM: Jayjay, just/

JAYJAY: That on the palest dusty leg hairs, God can hide. *(To Farah.)* Give it here.

Farah stretches her legs out towards him.

JEM: Farah, cut it out.

Farah looks at Jem while Jayjay touches her leg hairs with the outside of his lips.

JAYJAY: Jem, baby girl, baby rat/

FARAH: *(To Jem.)* Yeah, baby rat. Look.

JEM: Fuck off.

JAYJAY: That God can be divine. That on the palest dusty leg hairs/

FARAH: You see God. *(Pause.)* Jem –

JAYJAY: That God can hide. And when the wheat is high, you are low. Just lying there/

JEM: Just lying there/

JAYJAY: And that's where I like you best, God. Yes. That's where I like you best.

He stands up and wrangles the girls into a group hug.

And out here where it is so vast, where I come from so many places that did not have God. That seemed empty at first, but you and I arrived together. Roomies, at last.

I won't stop doing your work, putting those systems on the fields. On feeding and taking care of all of the animals here on our farm, and in the grass and the house.

They all kneel, hands in prayer.

JAYJAY: Thank you for the strength and the wisdom. And again for leaving me alone about your weak-assed son. I know you won't regret it. We will be here and what we can find, what we can make, will rise up. Amen.

Jayjay drops to his knees, he falls forward, and places his forehead to the ground. Slowly he rises and exits.

SCENE 11

Jem and Farah are still in their kneeling prayer position.

FARAH: I love the part where they told you what you had to say.

JEM: Tell me again.

FARAH: Do you want me to?

They stand up.

JEM: Yes, please.

FARAH: Okay, are you ready now?

JEM: Yes. Come on. Tell me.

FARAH: You should do the whole part.

JEM: Why not? I feel like I have some electricity in me. I can run. I'm ready.

Jem starts to run around.

FARAH: You. Hey. You. You're an eternal first-year. Forever.

JEM: Okay.

FARAH: But you're excited 'cause that means they like you, right?

JEM: Yes, Farah. It was good. I was happy. Tell me the part.

FARAH: Okay. Then this is what you have to say.

JEM: Yeah?

FARAH: I feel good. I feel mean. I feel strong.

JEM: I feel good.

FARAH: Yeah. I feel mean.

JEM: I feel mean.

FARAH: I feel strong!

JEM: I feel strong. *(Pause.)* I feel good. I feel mean. I feel strong.

FARAH: Every time you run.

JEM: I feel good.
I feel mean.
I feel strong.

FARAH: Until we tell you to stop.

JEM: I feel good.
I feel mean.
I feel strong.

FARAH: Is that all you've got?

JEM: I feel good.
I feel mean.
I feel strong.

Jem stops running, they both face forward.

JEM and FARAH: I feel good.
I feel mean.
I feel strong.

I feel good.
I feel mean.
I feel strong.

FARAH: You are so lucky!

JEM: Yeah. I know. I think it was good for me.

FARAH: Look at you now.

JEM: You look at me.

FARAH: I am, idiot.

JEM: I hate you.

FARAH: You wish.

SCENE 12

The girls are asleep on the rug. Jayjay enters and stands there. He starts breathing really heavily for kind of a while. He paces in a stylized kind of pace. He takes his sweater off. He takes his sneakers off. He takes his sweatpants off. He just wears sport shorts.

JAYJAY: Hey pups. Storm's brewin'.

Farah starts to wake. Jem sleeps.

JAYJAY: I SAID, STORM'S BREWIN'.

FARAH: *(Kicking at Jem.)* Hey. Looks like a tornado's coming.

JEM: *(Waking up.)* I'm not into this right now.

JAYJAY: *(Picking his teeth and standing with one hand on his hip.)* Well, you better get into it.

FARAH: Jem.

JEM: *(Sleepily.)* Fuuuuck. Alright. I'm into it. One sec.

Jem rubs her eyes and her hair and wakes up some more. She stands up and gestures at the clothes that Jayjay took off.

JEM: *(To Farah, pointing at Jayjay's pile of clothes.)* Is that your "girlfriend"?

Farah responds with her part. Jayjay watches.

FARAH: Like you care. And there's a storm brewin'!!

JEM: Ahh. Okay. *(Pacing around a little bit.)* Hey – is that your girlfriend?

FARAH: Looks like a tornado's comin'.

JEM: *(To Farah.)* Is that your goddamn girlfriend?

FARAH: Where?

Jem kicks at the clothes as if they stand for a picture of "the girlfriend."

JEM: In that picture.

FARAH: Did you hear me? I said, looks like a tornado's comin'.

JEM: Oh goddamn hell. Where?

Farah peers out with her arm raised.

FARAH: Right out there, up east.

Jem stands next to Farah with her arm raised in the same way.

JEM: Holy shit. You're right. Storm's brewin'.

Jem starts to walk way, done with the scene.

JAYJAY: Hold it! Stay in that position. Keep it there.

Jem returns to the position with her arm raised.

JAYJAY: *(Prompting.)* She's pretty. Your girl/

JEM: I know it! I know what to say. *(To Farah.)* She's pretty. Your girlfriend is very pretty.

Farah brings her arm down.

FARAH: Do you even care that a storm's brewing?

JEM: No. Not right now. *(Puts her hands on her hips.)* Did you know all those girls in the pictures?

FARAH: Goddamn right.

JEM: Holy shit. There's a storm comin' and you knew everyone. All those girls out there. Every goddamn one.

FARAH: Yes.

Jem slaps Farah across the face.

JAYJAY: Good job.

Jayjay picks up his clothes and scoots.

FARAH: *(Bent over holding her face.)* You knew them too.

JEM: So.

Farah steps away.

FARAH: Sometimes I think I would have been a teacher, I just don't even know what grade.

SCENE 13

Jem and Farah standing on the rug.

JEM: Okay, okay. Seriously, ready.

FARAH: I'll start.

Farah walks out and then back in.

FARAH: You're supposed to look at me.

Pause.

JEM: *(Listening.)* I hear that fucker. He's coming.

FARAH: Sick. Do it quick.

Jem walks up to Farah and points her finger into her chest.

JEM: You drive long-haul?

FARAH: Sure do, little lady.

JEM: I'm coming with and I'm gonna need you to stop in/

Jayjay is crawling into the room acting incredibly cat-like.

JEM: Hold on. Damn it, he's here.

They watch him bat at a field hockey ball.

FARAH: Uhhhh.

JEM: Come on.

FARAH: I know, it's just like, his body is weird.

JEM: He wants it like that.

Jayjay has cat-crawled to the girls. He rubs his body and purrs on Jem's leg.

JEM: *(Petting Jayjay.)* What do you want, Jayjay?

He lies on his back and sticks his feet out.

JAYJAY: Meow. They're scaley.

FARAH: Retch.

JAYJAY: That's right nice of you, Farah. I'm gonna need you to get the scales off.

Farah gets a jar of nail polish and sits and starts painting Jayjay's toenails. Jem sits and does handwork on a pelt.

JAYJAY: Good morning out on the wheel. Real nice. Rows of progress. You girls would be real proud. Beans, chives, vibrations. Really like the developments. Sure-be-doo. Ahh. I pray real hard. And hoo – I pay now. Yes. I do. You getting that?

JEM: She got it.

Farah continues to paint Jayjay's toes.

JAYJAY: *(To Jem.)* You're not gonna like the sound of this, but I'd really like a little work on my ass. *(Does a massage hand gesture.)* Just a lil' rub. It gets so hot there in that kitchen and my ass get real red and tight.

JEM: It's the deep fryer.

JAYJAY: Hooo-oooo.

FARAH: Jayjay, your butt is like the sickest thing ever.

JAYJAY: Oh no lady. No, no it ain't. It is like a high wind. A high desert wind that blows in the tidings and brings cheer to those dark, sad places. That is my ass. Its glorious contours set to deflect and defend all we got here. And I know you know it. I know you know it.

JEM: *(Exiting.)* I'm gonna go make a wheatburger.

JAYJAY: My ass will deflect it.

Farah blows on his toenails one more time and stands up. Jayjay scoots out on his ass.

SCENE 14

Farah and Jem do a field hockey drill on the rug.

JEM: This is the scene.

FARAH: Yes.

Jem uses her stick as a microphone.

JEM: Alright. Boys and girls. We are coming to you live. From way, way out heeerrreee.

FARAH: Oh yeah.

JEM: And you know what, kitty cats? It's really great out here. And we got all the sounds you cravvvvve.

FARAH: Oh this is really good.

JEM: So, I want you to sit back and listen to the sounds you love.

FARAH: I want a sound I remember.

JEM: Well, SnailTail. We're taking requests. This is your Dreamtime Request Hour.

FARAH: Shit! Okay. I want that song you heard when the wind went by the bus window and you kept riding. And you didn't even know where it came from.

JEM: This early in the hour? Well, we give our girls what they want.

Farah claps her hand.

JEM: This is the story of freedom, of the future, of a return to before/

FARAH: This is my story.

JEM: Oh yes. This is my song. And my family tree/

JEM: And this is what these sounds make me do!

JEM and FARAH: And this is what these sounds make me do!
This is what these sounds make me do.

SCENE 15

Jem is alone.

JEM: I got there. I got back there and I just crouched down. I was sweaty. And I just crouched down behind that dumpster. And I took off my sweaty old headband. And I took off my underwear. I really wanted to feel clean and salty. It was that really pretty time of pre-night. When the lights of home burn really clarified. And laughing and dinner fill you up. I could hear all the clatter. Everyone at the bus. All the packing up. All the winning. And I could feel the grass on my butt. One piece poked up and it felt really sharp. And I looked down at my shoes, those sharp black cleats with purple stripes. They were really strong shoes. I could plant my foot and they would just like hold. I know what it's like to have important things around you. And to lose things. And to make the choices that cause you to lose those things. And the deep hollow center to that knowledge that is the anchor to a place like this. A working farm. I can't say I knew where I was going. And who I was coming towards. But I knew what I was leaving. *(Pause.)* Yeah. *(Pause.)* I was in my away uniform.

A long time passes. Jem eventually sits down on the rug. Farah walks out very slowly not making eye contact with Jem and sits down too.

SCENE 16

The girls lie on the rug not touching. They look very pale and strange. They both wear old t-shirts in different colors. They move their hands in small ways to touch the rug and their hair. A long time passes.

JEM: I want that one.

Her hand and arm barely gestures towards Farah's t-shirt.

FARAH: What? *(Pause.)* You can have it. I mean. *(Pause.)* Are you serious?

JEM: Yeah.

FARAH: Why?

JEM: It just looks really good on you.

Farah kind of laughs.

A long pause.

FARAH: Yeah.

JEM: Totally.

Long pause.

FARAH: Why are you saying that?

Long pause.

JEM: Well, I'm *(long pause)* serious.

Long pause.

FARAH: Can you hear me breathing?

They both listen for a long time.

JEM: I think so. Something's happening.

FARAH: Yeah. *(She whispers some.)* The molecules are moving I think. That's what it is.

JEM: *(Kind of whispering too.)* But like not moving –

FARAH: Yeah.

Pause.

FARAH: The dust. It's on the march.

Long pause.

JEM: How do we know this is happening.

FARAH: I can hear everything.

JEM: Yeah. Hold on.

FARAH: I know. *(Long pause.)* Right.

JEM: Move less.

FARAH: Yes.

JEM: They go in and out.

FARAH: Those molecules.

JEM: I feel like it's not weird.

FARAH: But we should hear something.

JEM: Listen.

Long pause.

JEM: There's no sound. *(Pause.)* I think I can hear it.

Farah crawls towards Jem.

FARAH: Yeah. It's flat.

Farah lies curled up kind of with Jem. They both stay there and their eyes close. A white noise sound happens low and quick. Pause. Jem moves her hand over the braided rug.

JEM: Out here. The wind moves things.

SCENE 17

The girls are asleep on the rug. Jayjay comes out and stands there.

JAYJAY: So yeah, my ass. So, the goddamn what. I don't got no one touching it and getting in my grill this way. You know. And I can handle that. I do handle it. I use it. And I've found other ways to use it. And these two don't even know what is. What is what. They're like those sleeping dogs in those big down low southern countries, the dry hot, sweet ones, those places, sleeping right there on the pavement that wraps round. Real dirty hot cement. And those dogs with their softest fur and their heartbeats. And lemme tell you they gotta be covered in dust. Damn covered in it. Holy dust. Damn it, yes, I recognize the contradict of that, but in my moments I know those dogs are dirty and soft. You know it. They goddamn are. Those places are goddamn dusty and filthy and hot sauce floats through the air. Oh yeah. That's what those big, southern special lands are like. Real contained and different. And hot and dirty as dust on a weedass. *(Laughing.)* Fuck. A weedass. I do have a laugh. And these two. Shit. *(Long pause.)* I know what God says. This. *(Spreads his arms out slowly to encompass him, them, the space.)* This is love.

SCENE 18

Farah, Jem, and Jayjay all stand on the rug.

FARAH: *(To Jem.)* Now you tell me. The best story of all.

JAYJAY: Oldest story in the book. But it is a good one. Reason it's a classic.

FARAH: Right. Okay, go Jem.

JEM: I didn't make it the first year.

FARAH: You were cut.

JAYJAY: Kind of a loser right.

JEM: Yeah, I was cut.

FARAH: Then what happened?

JEM: I didn't stop. Forever. I just kept going. I got fully dressed. My underwear, a headband, those socks, the shoes, I had all the stuff. I was weak and small, but I got dressed. And I moved in and out. And I did not stop.

FARAH: And then?

JEM: Then I made it.

Pause.

I made it.

FARAH: Holy shit. You made it. Like think of that. You made it. All those people want to make it. And like you did. Others got dressed, and got ready. You had something. I can't believe it. Like, I can't believe it. That is what makes me the most proud of you and what I think of on the rug and how I fall asleep and why I – could stay here. You made it.

Pause.

I didn't make it, really.

JEM: You kind of did. *(Pause.)* You know things.

FARAH: Not really.

SCENE 19

The girls stand in the middle of the braided rug. Jayjay stands just back, eating oatmeal from a bowl and watching them.

JEM: This look means I love you.

She bites her lip.

FARAH: Do it again.

Jem does the look.

FARAH: Do it again. It's good.

Jem does the look.

FARAH: Do it again.

Jem does the look.

FARAH: Oh, do it again.

Jem does the look.

FARAH: Do it again.

Jem does the look.

FARAH: Do it again.

Jem does the look.

FARAH: Do it again.

Jem does the look.

FARAH: Please, do it again.

Pause.

JEM: I can't. I'm so tired.

Pause.

FARAH: Please.

End of Play

FAMILY

Characters and Setting

Mum, Agnes, a deposed third-tier faintly royal single mother (beautiful, regal, weary)

Lily, the older daughter, age 21

Frarajaca, the younger daughter, age 19

Sharky, male housemaid/musician

Rolf, family friend. No one ever knows if he's around or not.

Art Girls (Friends of Frara):

> **Cygon**, short and smart
>
> **Sharon**, her project involves coming out
>
> **Phillipa**, helping Sharon with her project
>
> **Bronstein**, focused and implacable
>
> **Michael Prelps**, swims laps in the family's heated, outdoor salt-water pool all day. He's like their pet.

They live in their own evergreened archipelago off the coast of somewhere. It seems like they might have been banished (from New England?). But it doesn't really matter, they still live in a sort of castle. On their grounds are a heated saltwater swimming pool and a snow globe that has an ice skating rink in it.

SCENE 1

In the great room. There is an oriental rug and an old wooden table stacked with antique wooden boxes of varied provenances. MUM stands on a covered highback chair stage left. She holds a lit cigarette regally in one hand and a megaphone in the other.

MUM: Get off the tiger head, Lily.

LILY is dressed in a pink ballerina skirt on top of a high-up tiger head.

LILY: No. I'm not gonna. I'm doing it. This is how I'm going to do it and you can't/

MUM: Not tonight. I just— Get out of there right now. I just had that wood spray-washed. It's completely/

FRARAJACA mopes through. She has ink on her face, mistakenly.

FRARAJACA: Where's that sucky thing? *(Makes a motion with her arm.)* I need it for my keyboard. There's crumbs everywhere in it.

LILY and MUM look sort of distractedly at FRARAJACA.

FRARAJACA: Unhhh. I hate everything.

FRARAJACA exits.

MUM: *(Calls after Frarajaca.)* This isn't my cigarette, sweetheart.

LILY has stepped off of the tiger head. She has some soot on her face.

She walks up the stairs to the bedrooms.

LILY: Mum. It's like whatever. She doesn't care. Are we having chips? With the lobster??

MUM: Of course.

LILY: *(Over the banister.)* Is Rolf coming?

MUM: No. Why would he?

SCENE 2

Lights up on the girls up in their bedroom. FRARAJACA is doing an art project on her bed. LILY stands and brushes her hair by the window.

FRARAJACA: So, what are you gonna do?

LILY: About what? Dying? I don't even care at this point. *(She brushes.)* I don't know. It's just. I want it to be dramatic you know. Like a pioneer. And I'm not just gonna go through with/

FRARAJACA: You're so spoiled.

LILY: Shut up.

FRARAJACA: You are.

LILY: That's rich coming from you. *(She keeps brushing her hair.)*

FRARAJACA holds up her video camera and tapes herself saying: "This is the thing about horse hair..."

FRARAJACA: Shit – no. Okay.

She holds the camera up again and tries a different approach: "Horse hair has been used throughout history as..."

FRARAJACA's horse hair improv with her video camera continues for a bit.

FRARAJACA: *(Putting camera down.)* Forget it. *(Pause.)* What's Michael doing?

LILY: *(Looking out the window, down at the pool.)* Backstroke it looks like. Or a drill, maybe. I don't know. Who cares? I've got other stuff to worry about besides art. And Michael. You're not about to be force-impregnated. It sucks.

FRARAJACA: Yeah, it is kind of weird. But, is it like totally gonna happen?

LILY: Ummm, yeah. If Mum has anything to say about it. She lives for this shit. It's like her dream. The whole lineage. And the fact that we were even gifted the sperm in the first place. She's not gonna waste it.

FRARAJACA: It's so weird. *(Pause.)* I mean. Why don't you just get rid of it? Like, pour it down the drain or something?

LILY: I could never do that. I'm not that bad. I wish I could be. But I'm not that bad. It would. It would like tear her heart out. She's here. I mean half the days she stacks all the wood by herself, she hardly highlights her hair anymore, all those trips to the dump. I mean, just for us basically. And even if it's so messed up. I understand in these ways why it's important to her, I kind of do.

FRARAJACA: Do you think she wanted to have his baby herself?

LILY: Ewwww. No. It's just like. I don't know. It's. It's like the last vestiges of what she was. And they were. And all they had. All that old traditional stuff.

FRARAJACA: It is kind of a big deal.

LILY: I know, right. And he was really handsome.

FRARAJACA: I think he was gay.

LILY: Uuhhh! That's so dumb. Why are you so annoying? It doesn't even matter. Who cares. He's not even alive! It's just his sperm.

FRARAJACA: Yeah. That's the creepy part.

LILY: I don't know. It happens. You know that! Don't you remember Bobbie? From Synchronized Archery? 'Member, she had that amazing python luggage rack and those plastic cuffs at the summer dance? Remember? But then last fall she didn't go to Nationals and then hasn't been around at all since and I had heard her family had something also, so you know, she probably got *(Gestures to stomach.)* ...you know. *(Pause.)* And Mum, Mum's been waiting for this.

MUM is up in her attic smoking. She's stuffed the attic full of evergreen branches because she thinks it masks the smell of smoke.

And this is why she has a megaphone in the first place, so she can yell down into the rest of the house.

MUM: *(Into the megaphone.)* Lily. Lily. Honey. Get your ass up here. Please.

LILY: Shoot. Alright. I'm gonna go talk to her. *(Screams to Mum.)* Coming.

MUM: *(Into the megaphone.)* Is Michael down there? I can't find any clean rags. He needs to coordinate with Sharky over the laundry.

SHARKY plays a tune and sings: "Sh-aaaar-ky."

Pause.

FRARAJACA: *(To Lily as she's leaving the bedroom.)* Why can't we have sex with Michael?

LILY: Oh my god. Gross. You're so weird.

SCENE 3

LILY heads up into MUM'S attic smokehole.

LILY: What?

MUM: I was looking for your skate pom-poms.

LILY: Mum.

MUM: Aren't they up here?

LILY: Didn't you sell them? And why? I don't like those ones anymore.

MUM: Oh. I thought you were looking for them so I came to see if they were up here.

LILY: Mum.

MUM: They used to be. *(Long pause.)* Anyways, John Green Stables mentioned the Klondike's. I know what the Klondike's think, Lily. I've been involved with those asshole for years. I don't want anyone to tell them that you haven't taken Nureyev's sperm.

LILY: Fine.

MUM: I just don't want to talk about it with them. Okay. Let's not bring it up. That is all I ask/

LILY: Good. Great. Fine. Why would it even come up? I definitely don't want to talk about it. And they live in Helterskine. We never see them anyways.

MUM: I'm not the village idiot.

LILY: I know.

MUM: And they're just all over everybody's business.

LILY: Mum.

SCENE 4

MUM is in the kitchen. There's a woodstove, another oriental rug. She is microwaving something. FRARAJACA walks in. MUM takes out two mugs and hands one to FRARAJACA.

FRARAJACA: So I need to bring my new adopted parents something.

MUM: What are you talking about Frarajaca?

FRARAJACA: *(Preparing, then eating Nutella toast.)* I told you. Our entire class was adopted by Germany.

MUM: What? I don't understand.

FRARAJACA: Do we have any frozen waffles?

MUM: Wait a second. What the goddamn hell is that supposed to mean? Adopted by Germany? You have a family.

FRARAJACA: Yeah, I know, it's boring, but it's happening. *(Eats.)* I want real syrup. Do we ever have any? Where's Michael? Did he use it for tanning? Did he get a new bathing suit or something? I thought I saw a weird flag thing the other day. Where is he anyways?

MUM: Grocery shopping. He swam to the Mainland yesterday. So, please tell/

FRARAJACA: Is there any real syrup in the cellar?

MUM: I'm helicoptering to class with you next week. *(Pause.)* And I'm talking to your teacher. This is insane. Adopted by Germany?! What did Lindsay's mother say?

FRARAJACA: I dunno.

FRARAJACA leaves kitchen.

MUM: Those assholes.

SCENE 5

FRARAJACA is in her room.

FRARAJACA: *(On the phone.)* We can't rehearse in our garage. You'd have to stay out here for like a week and it's totally filled with crap. *(Pause.)* No, we don't even have a car. *(Pause.)* I don't know, it's just full of damaged art and fur heads. Just crap everywhere. *(Pause.)* Well! *(Pause.)* Well, it feels like this project is being held together by dreams right now and I want to feel like I actually live for something. *(Pause.)* Fine. *(Pause.)* Okay. *(Pause.)* Yeah. *(Pause.)* See you in a couple days. Byyyee.

LILY comes into the room.

LILY: When are you going to get rid of all of these stuffed animals?

FRARAJACA: Never.

Pause.

FRARAJACA: I'm just going to start doing my own art. I can't coordinate on these group projects with those spoiled brats from Argentina and the Baltics. It's stupid. Unnh! Besides I have an idea.

LILY: Like what? What are you going to make?

FRARAJACA: A gangbang.

LILY: What?

FRARAJACA: Like a gangbang.

LILY: "Gang" "bang"?

FRARAJACA: Gang. Bang.

LILY: Gangbang?

FRARAJACA: Yeah. Like an awesome one. Like the most beautiful version of it.

LILY: Oh my god, you don't even know what you're talking about.

FRARAJACA: Neither do you.

LILY: WHAT?? WHAT?? I am about to be impregnated with Rudolf Nureyev's frozen fucking sperm and become – and become a fucking mother!!! Just to make Mum happy, and you're saying I don't even know about gangbangs.

LILY's screaming and crying outburst eventually settles into slow, soft crying.

LILY: Don't tell me I don't know about gangbangs.

SCENE 6

MUM is smoking in the attic smokehole. She smokes for one minute while music plays. It is like an x-ray of a person in that moment. A beautiful, scary, honest moment of MUM by herself.

SCENE 7

MUM is coming down the stairs from the attic smokehole. A huge stuffed teddy bear, like four feet tall, comes flying down the stairs and nearly knocks her onto the cement floor beneath the stairs. MUM clutches the railing to save her life.

MUM: OH MY GOD. WHO DID THAT???? WHO THREW THAT BEAR DOWN THE STAIRS????

FRARAJACA: *(Crying.)* I did. But it was an accident. I didn't mean to.

MUM chases FRARAJACA all over the stage, until she reaches her and grabs her hair.

MUM: You could have killed me. You could have killed me.

FRARAJACA: I know. I know. I was just cleaning out my room. And I thought it was time to move some of that stuff out.

LILY enters.

LILY: What happened? Why are you crying?

FRARAJACA: I almost killed Mum. And it was an accident. And I didn't mean to. I just threw without looking and/

LILY: Threw what? Threw what?

FRARAJACA: The big brown bear—

LILY: From your room? What?

MUM: She could have goddamn killed me. If I hit the ground and/

LILY: Why did you just throw it down there? What are you thinking? Are you kidding/

FRARAJACA: I don't know, I/

LILY: You were just going to throw down it into the basement? Oh my god!

MUM: I can't believe this. I'm still shaking.

LILY: I know.

Really long pause. Music. The three of them look at SHARKY.

LILY: Why are we so screwed up?

Long pause.

MUM: *(Turns her head towards the girls.)* I left those baggies upstairs. *(Heads back up to the attic.)*

FRARAJACA: Everyone is so stupid. And P.S. I hate everyone.

LILY grabs one of her boobs and looks down at it. She looks over at FRARAJACA.

SCENE 8

FRARAJACA is upstairs in her bedroom.

FRARAJACA: *(Yelling down.)* Mum! Mum! Where is that cartouche that Old Man Wang gave me? Mum!! I need that little Egyptian necklace he got me – I need it for our rap mix – Mum! Mum!!

LILY comes in.

LILY: *(Yelling up.)* Shut up! She's not here. God. And don't fucking take my cartouche!!

FRARAJACA: Are you serious? Are you serious? I CAN'T use your cartouche, idiot. I need it to spell my name – your hieroglyphics are totally different! What's your problem?

LILY: What do you think, Frarajaca?

FRARAJACA: Well, take your bad attitude out of here. Cause my friends are coming over and I don't want you lurking around being a bitch.

LILY: Fuck off.

LILY exits.

SCENE 9

The ART GIRLS enter. FRARA is doing field hockey drills and singing "Raccoons in the Basement."

The girls have bags and various girl detritus. They enter singing on the second chorus of "Raccoons."

The following brief sections, Part 1 and Part 2, can kind of overlap.

Part 1:

PHILLIPA is braiding SHARON'S hair on the couch. SHARON is playing a handheld electronic game.

SHARON: So, Phillipa.

PHILLIPA: Yeah.

SHARON: Oh, nothing. Forget it.

PHILLIPA: What baby?

SHARON: Are you really gay?

PHILLIPA turns around, sweetly thinks before speaking, maybe sweetly strokes SHARON'S cheek.

PHILLIPA: I'm… really open.

SHARON: Cause right now. *(Pause.)* I feel like I'm gonna love you so hard. Forever.

Sweet pause.

PHILLIPA: Are you serious?

Short sweet pause.

SHARON: I want to be.

PHILLIPA leans up and kisses SHARON on the cheek.

BRONSTEIN does some eye rolling. FRARAJACA just looks at them out the side of her eyes quickly (small eye roll maybe). CYGON smiles quickly at them.

Part 2:

BRONSTEIN: *(To Cygon.)* Yo Cygon. Did you wanna work the move or not?

CYGON: Yes, let's do it, I'm ready. Thanks, Bronstein.

BRONSTEIN: Did you decide if you're growing your hair out or not?

CYGON: Umm.

BRONSTEIN: *(Sizes her up.)* It is cute. But a little, I don't know, girl detective, or something.

PHILLIPA: You have great hair, Cygon.

SHARON: It's the best.

FRARAJACA: I think, if anything, you should get a Side Shanty Shave and keep the left side longer. But. Whatever.

BRONSTEIN: Yeah. Whatever. *(To Cygon.)* Let's dance. Snap it. Snap it. Snap it.

CYGON comes in on the third "snap it."

BRONSTEIN: And a 5, 6, 7, 8...

CYGON can't get the move.

BRONSTEIN: Cy! Come on. Please try to do this right.

CYGON: Okay. Okay. I can do it. One more time.

They line up next to each other. They do the move together.

CYGON and BRONSTEIN: A 5, 6, 7, 8...

BRONSTEIN: Good one.

They all start doing a dance sequence together.

FRARAJACA: *(As they are dancing.)* Sharon, I can see you out of my peripherals and you're clearing doing something modern when we're/

LILY walks in holding the family's Maine Coon Cat. FRARA kind of shushes her friends. LILY stands there.

CYGON: Hi Lily.

LILY: Hey.

THE OTHERS: Hi Lily.

FRARAJACA: We're kind of rehearsing. And stuff.

LILY: So.

FRARAJACA: Snap out of it.

LILY: You.

Pause.

SHARON: I like your cat.

Pause.

FRARAJACA: That's our cat. It's the family cat. It's not her cat.

Pause.

BRONSTEIN: Yeah. I'm so not into quibbling over the repressive ownership politics of soft things, i.e. cats. *(To Lily.)* Lily, do you wanna give us a critique?

Pause.

LILY looks at FRARAJACA.

LILY: Yeah, I could do that.

SHARON: You were the best dancer your year.

PHILLIPA: Your pas de deux with Mona Finkles at the Senior Spring Washout was like so fucking awesome.

LILY: Thank you. Yeah, I'll do the crit. Was that *(does a move)* what you're presenting?

FRARAJACA: No. It's just our audition tape piece for now. It's supposed to address global issues, transient patriarchal structures and western urbanization.

BRONSTEIN: And, if we feel like it, we can touch on avant-garde agency in fluid sub-cultures.

CYGON: I think we should try to put that in there.

LILY: Okay, so/

FRARAJACA: We, of course, also want to insert some "street" into it. You know? That's important.

LILY: Yeah, totally. Okay, well, just start at the/

Singing is heard off stage: "I want to reach to the highest heights. I want to swim to the highest rock."

The girls stop. Eventually ROLF who was singing enters. He wears riding boots, a cool kind of punk t-shirt with a horse wearing sunglasses tucked into jodhpurs, and a rabbit fur bomber jacket.

FRARAJACA: Hey Rolf.

LILY: Hi Rolf.

FRARAJACA: Okay, Rolf, these are my friends, you may have met them or something.

ROLF: Girls!

GIRLS: Hey Rolf.

FRARAJACA: Guys, this is Rolf.

ROLF mumble/sings more of "Reach to the Highest Rock": "I'm gonna swim to the highest rock..."

Noone knows what to do. Rolf stops singing.

ROLF: Lily. You look great. Your mother told me your staying home this summer and preparing. Are you good?

LILY: Yeah, I'm okay.

ROLF: It means a lot to her. You are very good daughter.

LILY: I guess so.

ROLF: Where is your mother?

FRARAJACA: Where is Mum?

LILY: MUM!!!! Rolf's here!

FRARAJACA: Oh shit. Wasn't someone supposed to pick her up at the Mini Renn? She was ordering the hooves for the back room. And getting that lacquer. Fuck. I totally forgot. Michael swam her over, but she wanted someone to bike out and get her after in the cart. Oops.

LILY: I think the Shilalees were going also. I'm sure they can give her a ride back.

CYGON: Mr. Shilalee is hot.

PHILLIPA: Are you serious?

BRONSTEIN: Is he still a banker?

ROLF: Frarajaca, did you ever figure out the right solution for that horse hair installation? Rodney thinks he can get his hands on some tanning sparkle and just back a vat up to the carriage house next time I'm out if/

FRARAJACA: Oh, yeah. I actually figured out a resin-based solution for Equine Tails 2700, *(High-fives one of the girls: "Resin!")* but it's super nice of you to offer, ummm, Rolf, we're just gonna, like, we totally have to practice now.

ROLF: Alright. I need a gimlet actually like a shot in the ass. And just to sit for a bit. Hot air balloons! We did a half-tip over the Smoky Barnacle in the Schwelters Range and I didn't think I'd live to see the/

FRARAJACA: Rolf.

ROLF: *(Exiting.)* Don't mind if I do.

FRARAJACA: Alright. I've got some stuff.

FRARAJACA starts grooving. The other girls kind of feel it. SHARKY accompanies with some music.

FRARAJACA: Okay, okay. On your knees. *(Does animal crawl-move.)*

CYGON: I love it.

SHARON: Totally. *(Getting down.)* Meow.

PHILLIPA: Meow.

BRONSTEIN is standing there doing weird claw hands.

LILY: It's pretty good.

FRARAJACA: You think that's good? Check this out...

FRARAJACA, LILY and ART GIRLS sing "My Cartouche."

Hey baby, hey
Have you seen my cartouche?
You know what I mean
And I'm feeling kind of loose
Hey baby have you seen my cartouche?

Spell it, spell my name
Spell my name, spell it
Spell it, spell my name
Spell my name in hieroglyphics
Spell it, baby, on my cartouche

(I said spell it)
I said spell it

Beautiful gangbang
Beautiful gangbang
Beautiful gangbang
Beautiful gangbang

We be goin' really fast
We be goin' really far
We be goin', we be goin'
We be goin' to the art fair
Spell it baby on my cartouche

(Beautiful gangbang)

This is my family and these are my friends
This is my cartouche
Where the bird means "N"
This is my family
These are my friends

Beautiful gangbang
Beautiful gangbang
Beautiful gangbang
Beautiful gangbang

Instrumental Break

This is my family and these are my friends
So spelling means love
Then family means forever
Read it baby on my cartouche
My cartouche for any weather

This is love
This is love

(This is love)
(This is love)

Beautiful gangbang
Beautiful gangbang
Beautiful gangbang
Beautiful gangbang

FRARAJACA: Spell my name in hieroglyphics!!

High-five-ing and jumping.

SCENE 10

FRARAJACA runs into the kitchen. MUM is slicing cheese. LILY is eating.

FRARAJACA: Oh my god. Oh my god. I got in. We got in. Our group project. They accepted us. We're going to the Art Fair. Holy shit! I cannot believe this!

MUM: Oh, Frara. Congratulations.

LILY: *(Eating cookie dough.)* How're you gonna pay for it?

FRARAJACA: What are you talking about? Why are you asking that right now? Shut up. Mum, I'm gonna totally need to get ready. It's such a good opportunity. I've gotta talk to those girls.

MUM: You're going to need that roller bag. It's downstairs.

FRARAJACA: I think I need a new bag. And I want to get my hair blown out.

LILY: Why?

MUM: Frara, you need to focus here.

FRARAJACA: I know! I know. I'm sorry! It's just like, oh my god. I've totally gotta call them. Cygon's like about to get like some library code tattooed on her arm and she totally has to wait until after this. Eeee! I can't believe it. We're totally gonna be art stars!!

FRARAJACA exits.

LILY starts crying.

MUM: Lily.

LILY: It's so not fair. It's so not fair!

MUM rubs her hair.

MUM: Lily. Frara doesn't have what you have.

LILY: I don't care. I don't care. Can't you see that? I don't want to be a mum yet. It's so stupid. I can do it later.

MUM: Lily. Listen to me. We only have the four months left that Rudy's spermicetti is still good. And there is no reason everything you want can't happen later.

LILY: But Mu/

MUM: It's why we sent you to the Putney Hill Academy. And gave you all these opportunities. *(Pause.)* It is an honor our family received. And it's the only thing I've asked of you. You played Clara when you were seven, you danced Giselle at fourteen. Your Dew Drop Fairy – the youngest at the Malovksy! – won seven straight competitions. You will be the mother of Nureyev's only daughter. And you will be a lovely, lovely Mum. *(Pause.)* And we will be here to help you.

LILY has still been eating. She's slowly calmed down. Sniffling a little as her crying eases.

LILY: Okay. Okay.

MUM rubs LILY'S hair.

LILY: But while she's getting ready for her big fat art trip, I don't want to talk about it with Frara anymore. *(Sniffs.)*

MUM: That's fine. Let's move on.

FRARAJACA comes back in.

FRARAJACA: Mum.

MUM: Yes, dear?

FRARAJACA: I need to get all those images photoscribed before we leave I just realized – can we go across the lake tomorrow maybe?

MUM: I think so. Rolf should be out. If I can't go, he can take you in the speedboat. But before you girls do anything else today, I do need you both to help me pick up some sticks.

LILY: Now?

FRARAJACA: I don't understand picking up sticks.

MUM: There are sticks all over the driveway from that wind tunnel last week. And into the side sweep.

LILY: I know, but they're sticks. They belong outside. That's where sticks are.

FRARAJACA: Yeah. There are so many sticks out there. Like trees and sticks. That's what's outside. Michael already got the sticks out of the pool.

MUM: The driveway looks like crap. It'll take a half an hour.

LILY: But no one comes over. No one even sees. Who cares then?

MUM: I asked you girls to help me with some sticks.

LILY: Fine.

FRARAJACA: I just have to put my cleats on then.

FRARAJACA run upstairs.

LILY: It's so typical. She always gets out of it.

MUM: Lily, please.

LILY: *(Standing up.)* No Mum – just – oh – don't you understand anything? Ever? Why is it always me? Why always me? I do not understand.

MUM: Lily. Don't you think there are a lot of things that I don't want to do? That I've had to make choices I didn't want to make? That is life, Lily. Doing what you don't want to do. For the people you love. *(Pause.)* Do you girls want a roast chicken for dinner? I still have those greens from Rolf's hog tie.

LILY stares at her.

LILY: I'm gonna go pick up sticks.

FRARAJACA calls down from upstairs.

FRARAJACA: Mum! Those girls are gonna come over tomorrow. We have to work on the project. I said they could come here, okay? So I just need to call Bronstein back and tell her to bring the slide projector – okay? Maybe I can go to the photo place after.

MUM: That's fine, Frara. But now you need to help your sister.

LILY: *(From off.)* Fuck all of you!

FRARAJACA: *(Yelling.)* Fuck you!

MUM: GIRLS!

SCENE 11

SHARON sits on the couch in the great room. PHILLIPA brushes SHARON'S hair. CYGON and FRARA are working on a sculpture. BRONSTEIN has on headphones, working on a dance move.

CYGON: Hey, Frara.

FRARAJACA: Yeah?

CYGON: So, you know Rolf?

FRARAJACA: Yeah.

CYGON: Is he like your mom's partner or something?

FRARAJACA: No. *(Pause.)* I don't know. He's just around sometimes. Like a family friend. You know. I mean, god, I don't think there's anything physical. She's not like that.

PHILLIPA and SHARON snap to attention and look at each other.

PHILLIPA and SHARON: Do you think she's gay?

FRARAJACA: Relax. *(Pause.)* I don't know. And it doesn't even matter.

CYGON: Oh, this is interesting. What are her gender politics anyways? I mean. I think your Mom seems pretty straight. But remember that class, Matriarchal Identity After the Ice Age: Whose Your Mommy? Yeah. After that, I couldn't stop thinking about how these women urgently need to self-define.

PHILLIPA: Yeaaah. And her hair's... not that gay.

SHARON: I love her hair though. It's so luxurious. I would be so excited if she was gay. That was a totally awesome class actually, you're right, Cygon.

CYGON: I just think it would be super interesting to get her to talk about, like, island-based domesticity and queer signifiers or something. I mean – this house is like a mu/

FRARAJACA: Cygon. Shut it. Can we please not talk about my mom right now.

CYGON: But then, if you consider, womb-based autonomy...

why would she care so much about Lily having that baby…?

FRARAJACA: That has nothing to do with anything. My mom is like in her own world. Clearly. We need to focus. We have to figure out this project for the art fair. We have the gangbang thing laid out – we'll figure the rest there – but we need our interpretive dance section. We leave in two days, girls.

SHARON: Oh, damn. Speaking of… everything! Philippa, did you tell your mum you didn't need to get your own room there? That we were sharing – eeeh!

PHILLIPA stands up.

PHILLIPA: Sharon. It's not a question of telling her I'm in love with you, if that's what you're implying. That's not even a question, okay? It's, I was thinking of … just getting the money anyways. And investing in some awesome punk records. The Latvian scene is supposed to be totally rad and maybe stocking up on a bunch of tubes of that dark red lipstick they have there. You know, like that Latvian movie star, Skittzie, always wears in her pictures. Uh, god, I love Skittzie.

SHARON: Oh yee-aah. You're so smart. Skitzzie is so cool. My mom's being a total penny-pincher.

FRARAJACA: Alright, we have to talk about this project. But the Skitzzie lipstick isn't a bad idea for our whole look.

SHARON: And, there's gonna be girls from like, everywhere, there.

FRARAJACA: That's why we have to get our shit together.

PHILLIPA: So, you guys, Sharon has this idea.

SHARON: Well, I kind of do.

FRARAJACA: Alright, we don't have a lot of time here.

CYGON: Briiiing it.

SHARON raps "Robots, Birds, Books and Bikes." BRONSTEIN provides back-up.

Hey
Hey
Hey

(Turn it up)
(Turn it up)

Get ready
Get ready

Oh yeah
Here's the thing
Here's what I'm gonna say
I might look pretty
But I'm ready to play

I got my girl
And I got my hair
I get straight A's in science
Like I care

After school
It's like what's the fuss
I don't need a scooter
I'll take the bus

Cause I'll sit with my girl
And I'll sit real fine
Hey everybody
Look. She's mine

Oh yeah
Oh yeah
Oh yeah

So I had tell my mum
Hey, I'm gay
She don't care
She don't play

She said, Hey little honey
Hey little miss
That's two princesses!
Give your Mum a kiss

So like
Robots, birds, books and bikes
Ballet, jazz, hot pants and tights
Bring it all over
Bring it all here

Uh – huh
Uh - huh

Holla
Holla

Uh – huh
Uh - huh

Holla
Holla

Ah-ah-ah-uh-ah-uh-ah-ah

Holla
Holla

Robots, birds, books and bikes
Break it on down
Break it down nice

(ice ice)

FRARAJACA: Well, it's not awful.

PHILLIPA: It's kind of transcendent.

CYGON: Let's make steps then.

SHARON sings. They dance. They are caught up in making dance, when BRONSTEIN takes her headphones off. They stop.

BRONSTEIN: So, for graduation. I'm getting a tattoo.

FRARAJACA: I'll give you a tattoo. I'll design it.

BRONSTEIN: I don't think so.

FRARAJACA: What? Are you kidding? My designs have won the Contoocook River Summer Sparklers Award every year. That's like the highest award for stuff made off-season.

BRONSTEIN: So. I just don't know, how, like, mystical your stuff can be. You know.

FRARAJACA: Mystical?? Bronstein. What are you even talking about?

BRONSTEIN: I'm just thinking, if I'm gonna mark my body, I want it to be mystical, spiritual, and relevant.

FRARAJACA stares at BRONSTEIN.

FRARAJACA: Oh my god! Have you even read my Artist Statement? That's exactly what I'm interested in! Forget it.

BRONSTEIN: I actually asked Cygon to design it.

FRARAJACA: What?

CYGON: Really?

BRONSTEIN: *(To Frara.)* I just don't know how religious you really are.

FRARAJACA: What? We used to be First Congregationalists.

BRONSTEIN: And?

FRARAJACA: The church got wormroot. And it totally rotted. *(Pause.)* We just have Solstice Square Dance here now. It's easier for Mum and everything. *(Pause.)* You know what, I don't even care. I'm gonna go log our audio samples. You guys can just – whatever.

FRARAJACA exits.

CYGON does a shimmy next to BRONSTEIN. Music pumps up a bit.

CYGON: So, what are you thinking of for your tat?

BRONSTEIN: Well. Spiritual and totally tasteful. I really liked that skateboard logo you made in screenprinting last semester.

CYGON: The braided unicorn furs? Or the Interior Wolf Mask?

BRONSTEIN: I want it to be my initials made of unicorn fur–and I want it to look like there's really good texture.

CYGON: Lower back? *(Gestures.)*

BRONSTEIN: Ughh. No. That's like, so, North America. Right here. *(Gestures to her inner forearm.)* For when I pray.

CYGON: Totally.

LILY enters holding the Maine Coon cat.

LILY: Where's Frara?

PHILLIPA: Freaking out. Or something.

SHARON: I think she's stressed.

LILY: Whatever. I'm making fish sticks. Do you guys want any?

ART GIRLS: Yes.

They start to head to kitchen.

CYGON: Where's Michael?

SHARON: Can we watch your ballet video, Lily?

ART GIRL parade/exit with chatter.

SCENE 12

FRARAJACA is in the great room. LILY gets a lemonade out of the refrigerator and walks through the room.

FRARAJACA: So, what did you think of those ideas?

LILY: Which ones?

FRARAJACA: The ones I said before.

LILY: Oh. *(Pause.)* They're fine.

FRARAJACA: It's just going to be/

LILY: Well, it doesn't/

FRARAJACA: What? What do you mean? Do you even get what I'm talking about?

LILY: Well, it's just from my perspective… *(Pause.)* Uhh. No, I guess, I just. I don't get it. I don't get it. I don't totally get the ideas.

FRARAJACA: Oh my god. Nobody understands anything!

LILY: Do you really know? I mean. Okay. Okay, those are pretty ideas. It's a cool concept, but it just feels sort of superficial, like coming from the outside. Like you're just trying to have an idea, but you don't actually have an idea.

Pause.

They look at each other.

FRARAJACA: It would be great if you could die.

LILY stands up and starts to walk away.

FRARAJACA: And, you're going to be the worst mom ever!!

SCENE 13

MUM is in the attic smokehole. She calls down to LILY on the megaphone.

MUM: Lily, take the Chop Suey out of the freezer.

LILY: Sick.

MUM: That's what we're having for dinner.

LILY: Sick. *(Pause.)* I'm not hungry. We all had a snack.

MUM: Are those girls still here? Are they eating?

LILY: No. They went with Frara to watch Michael swim under the log flume. *(Under her breath.)* It's so stupid. *(To Mum.)* I don't think they're coming back.

MUM lights another cigarette. Inhales deeply.

MUM sings "Stonewalls of My Heart."

Hey, don't forget your cleats
Do you have a hat?
I'll cut your hair
I'll cut your hair

Be there for you
For you

In the places so deep and real
When you don't even know
That's when I am here
For you

Hey, here's your card
I thought of you
This color too

Down in the playhouse
Up in the garage
Stop, kitties crossing
The stonewalls of my heart

Build em up
Build em up
Build em up
And build em down

The stonewalls of my heart
Of my heart
Of my heart

Wood by the woodstove
Means we're warm and loved
Blankets on the bed
Snow falls from above

Pine cones, butter churns
And love love love
Love love love

Down in the backyard
Up in the garage
Stop, kitties crossing
Stonewalls of my heart

Build em up
Build em up
Build em up and build em down

The stonewalls of my heart

She picks up her megaphone. The instrumental continues.

(Into the megaphone.) Lily. Lily. Come down here, please.

LILY stops dancing.

LILY: Coming Mum.

LILY runs up to the attic smokehole.

LILY: Mum. Mum. I love you.

LILY hugs MUM, who has hastily put out her cigarette. The remaining smoke floats around them.

MUM: I love you too. *(Long pause.)* You're very beautiful.

LILY: No, I'm not.

MUM: Yes, you are.

MUM starts singing. LILY joins in:

Down in the backyard
Up in the garage
Stop, kitties crossing
Stonewalls of my heart

Build em up
Build em up
Build em up and build em down

The stonewalls of my heart

SCENE 14

MUM and ROLF are in the kitchen.

MUM: What did you wrap that meatloaf with, Rolf?

ROLF: *(Sings something.)*

MUM: Rolf. Was that a wheat wrap or was there more flake? *(Rubs her fingers together on one hand to illustrate "flake.")*

ROLF: It was a ham wrap, Agnes.

MUM: Ohhh. That's right. God, that was delicious.

They both work on hor d'oeuvres for a while. Some dance steps as they maneuver the kitchen. Some humming. ROLF sings.

MUM: It's nice to have you here, Rolf.

ROLF: Thank you Agnes, it's nice to be here. *(Pause.)* I can't do any ironing though. I hurt my wrist.

MUM: Oh, no no. That's fine.

SCENE 15

LILY and FRARA are upstairs.

LILY: Frara.

FRARAJACA: Yeah?

LILY: I did it.

FRARAJACA: What??

LILY: Yeah. I did it. I'm freaking.

FRARAJACA stares in horror.

FRAJACA: It's okay. It's okay. Lily. It's gonna be good. *(Pause.)* Do you wanna look at my book of huge cathedrals? Here, lie down.

FRARAJACA brings her book to LILY and places it in her hands. LILY is frozen. FRARAJACA gently lays her back onto the pillows and lies down with her.

SCENE 16

LILY: *(From off-stage.)* Mum. *(Pause.)* Mum. *(Pause.)* Mum. *(Pause.)* Mum!! Mum!!!! Where are you?

MUM: *(Yelling down from the attic.)* Looking for the roller bag for your sister. Coming down. Just a second.

LILY: *(Walking into the kitchen.)* God.

MUM: Oh honey. Lily. I'll be right down.

LILY starts making brownie mix from a pink box.

LILY: Well. Old Man Wang is coming over. He just called.

MUM: Oh, jesus christ. What the goddamn does he want?

LILY: I'm making brownies.

MUM comes down the stairs with the megaphone in hand. Totally smells like cigarettes.

MUM: I'm too busy for this today. What does Old Man Wang want?

LILY: Did you find the bag?

MUM: No. I didn't find the bag. I know exactly where it is though. *(Goes back up into attic as she talks.)* Did you talk to Frara?

LILY: I don't understand why the bag is so hard to find.

MUM: *(Offstage/on the megaphone.)* Did you take your shots?

LILY: Yes. Why do you think I'm so STARVING!?

MUM: *(Offstage/on the megaphone.)* Sharky's going to have to help out here.

SHARKY plays a pointed melody.

(To Sharky.) There's the wood stove chimney, the hole in the pool, and you need to give Michael a rub. *(Pause.)* Can you help with some of this today, Lily?

LILY: I'm so depressed, Mum.

MUM: I've been depressed for 31 years.

Pause.

LILY: Can you ask Old Man Wang for more of those blue eye drops? *(Pause.)* Didn't they make my eyes look so blue, Mum?

MUM: I actually think Frara should take the Easel bag. I know you girls love that Lame Kitten thing – but the wheels stick. She doesn't need to deal with that.

LILY: I'm starving.

FRARA enters with her luggage.

FRARAJACA: Alright, I'm outtie.

MUM: Honey. Will you call as soon as you get to Skilkiestein? Boobar said he can send a car to get you girls to the hostel. Are you wearing that? You look like a hooker.

FRARAJACA: Mum! Thank you for the car set-up. And I'll totally call when we land. Bye, Lily.

LILY: Bye.

FRARAJCA: I'll get you something at the Lada store. Do you want fur cuffs?

MUM: Please save your money, Frarajaca. I'm not kidding around. This trip is a huge opportunity and you can't go crazy in those shops.

FRARAJACA: *(To Lily.)* I'll get you something.

LILY: I don't care. Have fun. Bye.

FRARAJACA: I love you guys. Bye.

SCENE 17

LILY sits on the couch holding a cigarette. She walks to the bedroom, picks up the video camera and returns to the couch. She holds the camera up and speaks into it, holding the cigarette.

LILY: I'm not gonna smoke it. I'm preggers. Or at least in a like a minute or something I'll be pregnant, because I have been inseminated now and the egg might actually be in process right at this moment or something. Besides, I hate smoking. I think it's disgusting. It just seems like a waste of work. All those hours at the barre, the ballet barre, all the plies, the sashays, the chantes, the extensions, smoking would just be like stupid when you've done all that work… Although. I have always thought that smoking made certain women or certain moments feel inexorably glamorous and important.

Like on our sleepaway cruises during Fall Crush when I went for ballet, I would sometimes hold an unlit cigarette in my hand – some girl always had one – like this – and lean lightly against the railing of the ship. And let my hair blow across my face. And I'd have a wrap sweater on over like a pale blue leotard. And those thickish pink tights with a backseam, you know, with those black nylon pants over them bunched up at my knees. And I would feel like in that moment, leaning into the salty wind with my sore muscles, and my long neck, and clutching bobby pins in my pale fingers… I would think that this is everything. This is everything. There is all this ocean here. See. And

I am here because I work really, really hard at something. I practice. And I am good at it. And this – me being here wearing my tights and my sweater and my bobby pins – what you only wear if you are a dancer – is everything. And back in my room on the ship, in the clutter of like white towels and hot packs and elastic bands, were my pointe shoes. And they also stood for everything.

Moments walking on stonewalls, diving into waves, feeling very loved, or swimming, laughing so hard, millions of times with Frarajaca and our friends that were like perfect, but nothing was like getting that first pair of pointe shoes that Mum took me to get.

And there's nothing like finishing, even just a class, where you won, where your team won – where you just put all your work into something that hit every mark – like scoring three goals in one half – but you're not really scoring goals, you're just dancing – but the hardest dance– because ballet is very tough, you have to be completely prepared. And after, when you take your ballet slippers off. And you know, that nothing more is needed, because you had these goals that you worked so hard to achieve. And you realize that achieving them actually felt better than you could have even imagined. Something you thought would be the best thing that could happen to you was even better than that.

Now there is the possibility of giving what I had to someone else. Which is so strange, because how can I make sure the best things ever can even happen for someone else. But leaning on that rail on the ship where

I wanted to be – it mostly seems like why we exist in these families in the first place.

She sings a secion section of "My Cartouche"... "beautiful gangbang... we be going really fast...."

SCENE 18

LILY lies on her canopy bed reading French fashion magazines. There is a stuffed seal on the bed and an ornate dreamcatcher hangs down over the headboard. She has her pink cell phone next to her on speakerphone.

FRARAJACA: *(From the cell phone.)* I just need $70. *(Pause.)* Now!! *(She cries and screams.)* Just $70 so I can rent a place to store the project and the gecko. You're telling me you at least can't help with that?!

LILY: I just feel like you're not acting very tough or something. And I don't have any extra money right now. I want to take one more day trip before/

FRARAJACA: *(From the cell phone.)* Oh my god!!! You are such a bitch. These girls are like totally deserting me and I can't even find money to get back, let alone, get this thing up and running. AHHHHHH.

LILY: Where are you anyways? What's all that clacking?

FRARAJACA: *(From the cell phone.)* I'm getting a manicure.

LILY: *(Sitting up.)* Shut up!

FRARAJACA: *(From the cell phone.)* You shut up.

LILY: You don't have a dime to your name and you're getting a manicure.

FRARAJACA: *(From the cell phone.)* My cuticles are totally wrecked. They're basically bleeding.

LILY: Oh my god. You have so many problems. This is so stupid. I'm studying. I don't have time for this. Have you talked to Mum?

FRARAJACA: *(From the cell phone.)* Umm, no. What good would that do. She says she's broke of course. *(Pause.)* No one even misses me. And don't tell me I have problems!!!!

LILY: I hate this family. If Mum's broke why are the front steps being re-done in granite and why the hell is Michael Prelps still here? Who's paying his/

FRARAJACA: *(From the cell phone.)* Ohhhh. I miss it there. How's Michael?

LILY: How would I know? He's in the pool all day. His armpits reek of chlorine and he eats everything in sight. He's super boring. But whatever, he's swimming the Channel next week, I guess I could be a tiny bit more supportive. Mum's meeting Rolf there. Whatever. It's just. It's not that great here. And I'm super busy with school stuff, doctor visits, whatever, so can we talk later?

FRARAJACA: *(From the cell phone.)* You don't even know where I'm staying and you don't even care. I'm not talking to anyone in this family ever again. *(She hangs up.)*

LILY: *(To herself.)* Oh my god.

Pause.

LILY walks to her windowsill and looks out.

LILY: Hey. Michael. *(Pause.)* Hey. *(Pause.)* Good job.

Long pause.

LILY: Michael. *(Pause.)* Frarajaca says hi.

SCENE 19

It is morning. MUM is in the kitchen, making coffee. LILY shuffles in.

MUM: Hi dear. You're up. I need to talk to you.

LILY: No.

MUM: Have you heard from Frara? I don't know when she's getting back and who, when, if anyone should row out to meet her. And when is she due back in school??

LILY: I don't know. She's out of money.

MUM: What. I gave her money. And Rolf – who does not have to do this type of thing – did too. I don't understand. Where did it go?

LILY: I don't know.

LILY pours some coffee and sits at the table.

LILY: She spent it on the project.

MUM: Oh goddammit. You're kidding me.

LILY: Mum.

MUM: I'm sorry. This is ridiculous. I don't understand this project and her "work." How are these other girls paying? That's what I'd like to know.

MUM is squeezing lemon juice into her hair.

LILY: What are you doing?

MUM: I can't afford highlights.

LILY: I hate her. Totally. But it's a pretty cool project. They've decided to try to re-create a reptile drug smuggling route through Amsterdam into the archipelago. Docu-Sparkle, they call it. It is cool the more I think about it. She's doing a smaller scale replication. Geckos instead of blood pythons. Synthetic uppers instead of hard coke. I don't know. She won't pull it off obviously. But if she did, it would be cool. And conceptually, I don't know, she's like, finally focused.

MUM: Lily. I –. *(Pause.)* Why. Why can't she just make rock paintings? There's a market for them. They'll sell! I have told her that for years. Those women at the Female Tree Society are constantly having the benefits and the auctions and that is what people buy. Rock paintings. I don't understand.

LILY: It's not art, Mum. She doesn't think that's art. Whatever. Anyways. Are you gonna send her money?

MUM: Lily, I don't have any. *(Pause.)* And I won't go back to Rolf and ask. He shouldn't have to do that. And art or not, she needs to be making something that sells. At this point.

LILY: What about her "adoptive" parents? Why don't they help.

MUM: Oh those assholes. Lily, Germany doesn't even have a goddamn answering machine. You can't live that way. She got that one Schnitzel Wreath, which Sharky ate or it shed, I don't know, and I have seen nothing else fruitful come out of that relationship. I doubt there's money there. I still don't understand what the school was thinking. It's/

LILY: Mum, I can't talk about this right now. I'm super tired and I have my own problems.

MUM: Alright, I'm going to the dump.

LILY: What are you taking to the dump now??

MUM: Frarajaca's old puppet theater that collapsed and has been under all the skis, those moth terrariums that were rotting in the pool house and my cotillion vases that those albino raccoons lived in for 14 years – it's disgusting. I need to clean up the cellar once and for all. And, if it rains later, Lily, I need you to pull the animal skins in from the deck, please.

LILY: Fine.

MUM exits.

SCENE 20

MUM and ROLF smoke in the attic smokehole. MUM wears a stylized safari jacket over her dress.

MUM: This edifice. This precipice. This point. This song. *(Long pause.)* I can't believe the goddamn dump was closed. That asshole.

ROLF: What artists do you like, Agnes?

MUM: What kind of question is that?

ROLF: Recording artists, Agnes? What recording artists do you like? *(Pause.)* Where do the girls get it? Their interest in all this ethereal captivity of spirit and emotion. Where do they get it? What's your favorite song, Agnes?

MUM: They get it from me. From me, Rolf. It's everything I gave them. All those trips to the Giant Milk Bottle, the books, the ballet, the balance beam, and black leotards. My old clarinet, the drum set, the dog stickers, Mt. Kearsarge, Pats Peak, and Annabelle Brooks. The twin beds, the bunk beds, the pink shag rug, the pale pink soft rug, the braided rug, the cats – Patchy, Cookie, Grey Guy, Fuzzy, Laalaa, and Four Paws, the dwarf hamsters, the glow fish, the full-size fish tank, the rocks for the bottom of the fish tank, Camp Conestayga, Cabin 13, the Old Road, the brown bog, ballet, tap, and jazz, Portsmouth Plantation, Strawberry Banke, whistles, passbacks, kilts, and yellow button downs. Tissue paper fish, gold leaf banisters, the Nutcracker, New London Barn Playhouse, Kimball's Pond, Kelly, Heather, Carl, and Rachel. G-S suits, goggles, turtle fur, and tiny nests. Christmas crowns, braids, and curls. Outfits, ironing, elastic bands, Wauwinet, horsehoe crabs, and Quidnet. Rope bracelets, purple pouches, lace knee socks, linen, orange sailboat bottoms, flipflops, moccasins, high-tops, scented Swatch watches, miniskirts, seagulls, and seaglass. The Western Woods, Rosemary's dresses, the green canoe, the back deck, lighthouses, leggings, tiny horses, small stables, and handknit sweaters. The tinfoil space ship, duck boots, flannel, state championships, windbreakers, wind pants, posters, pianos, mouse collections, nightlights, nail polish, and picture frames.

Those are all my favorite singers, Rolf.

MUM exits.

ROLF sings "This Place is Now":

I say, I say this place is now
I say, I say this place is now

I say, I say the time has come
In the walls and the floor boards
Here is now!
Now!
Is now

Set up the china
Plug in the tree
Vacuum the rug and believe in me

Smile to your right
Fork on the left
Folded napkin
Hand on my chest

Who's gonna say, who's gonna say?
Not a real prayer
But to welcome the day

I've seen you forever and I've seen you grow
Be set free,
To that you know

Plug in the china
Set up the tree
Vacuum the rug and dance with me

Hey, c'mon over
C'mon over here
Filled to the shingles with laughter and tears

High on the hill up the old road
This is a place far and old
High on the hill, we'll take my car
This is a place old and far!
Far!
So far.

How far have we come?
How long do we know?

(How far have we come?)
(How long do we know?)

SCENE 21

FRARAJACA and the ART GIRLS clamor home from the art show.

PHILLIPA: Okay, okay, one more time, the way the girls from Montreal did it.

They do the running jump dance pieces. Then huddle together and hug.

FRARAJACA: Thank you guys for everything. That was super fucking awesome. I love you.

SHARON: I love you guys too.

PHILLIPA: We're so lucky. We have friends like this.

CYGON: I can't wait until next year.

BRONSTEIN: I figured out something else. When Cygon draws those unicorn furs for my tattoo, she's gonna embed each of your names on one of the furs in Gaelic. Cause, you know, *(Pause.)* we actually probably won't be friends forever. But then I'll have you there.

CYGON: For when you pray.

BRONSTEIN: For when I make things.

PHILLIPA: You want me to sign your ass?

SHARON: Phillipa!

PHILLIPA: I'm just kidding. *(She hugs Sharon.)*

CYGON: Alright, my water taxi's here. I'm outtie. Later, dudes.

SCENE 22

FRARAJACA enters the great room with a load of luggage, holding a fluffy Maine Coon cat that wears rope bracelets on both front paws. Her dress looks a little bedraggled, but her hair is freshly blown out and her hat is super cute and stylish.

MUM sits in an antique chair wrangling with a roller bag.

LILY sits on an oriental rug eating a piece of yellow cake with pink frosting reading "Don Quixote."

FRARAJACA: Hiiiiii. *(Pause.)* I made it! I missed you guys. I'm so hungry. Do we have any turkey sausage? Mum, is there soy milk?? We need to go shopping. I want hummus.

MUM: Hi, honey. *(She keeps working on bag.)* I'm headed out for. It's been a bitch getting out of *(zipper breaks off)* Oh, goddammit! I need to get pliers downstairs.

FRARAJACA: Wait – I got another cat! He is so cute. This Persian cat breeder who got him from the Horn.

MUM: Oh goddammit. Frara, you're kidding. I don't need this.

FRARAJACA: Sharky – can you get him?

SHARKY brings in the cat.

FRARAJACA: Can you stand it?

MUM: *(Sighing.)* Frara. You are going to have to take care of these cats. I don't have the time or energy. I don't even know where… I'm getting those pliers. I'm glad you're back, honey.

MUM exits.

Pause.

FRARAJACA: Hi Lily.

Long pause.

LILY: How much did that cat cost?

SCENE 23

MUM sits in a little turtleneck in a big chair.

FRARAJACA walks downstairs and by MUM.

MUM: If you go to the bathroom, remember you can't flush the toilet, Frarajaca.

FRARAJACA: Uchh. I'm not. Why would I?

MUM: I'm just telling you. They're still not working. Make sure you listen to see if it's running and lift up the back. I can't afford to have the entire seasonal patrol over here replacing the septic.

FRARAJACA: I thought it was fixed.

MUM: They came out once, but it's never been right.

FRARAJACA: Those assholes.

MUM: Freakin' shit.

SCENE 24

FRARAJACA and LILY are in the great room. FRARAJACA holds an instrument, a recorder.

LILY: So you did see Skittzie. Was she really great?

FRARAJACA: Yeah, she was good. *(Pause.)* I'm gonna play a song for the baby.

LILY: Really?

FRARAJACA: Yeah. It's one from camp. It's called *Get Out of the Car*. Do you remember?

LILY: Oh my god! I haven't heard that in so long. Do you know how to play it?

FRARAJACA: Yeah. Totally. I am an art star. And that includes music sometimes.

LILY: I know.

FRARAJACA starts to play the song on the recorder. She stops.

LILY: It's almost like. *(Pause.)* Then we'll have another sister.

FRARAJACA: Weird.

LILY: What?

FRARAJACA: That's exactly what I was thinking.

FRARAJACA starts to play her recorder again.

All the ART GIRLS come in playing recorders. It is a beautiful chorus of recorders that goes into a dance they all do. ROLF enters and joins the dance.

MUM comes in distracted with a plunger.

LILY: Mum – do you remember this song?

FRARAJACA: Remember, Mum?

They dance close to MUM.

FRARAJACA: Do you remember?

LILY: We did it all the time when we were little.

FRARAJACA: Mum, do you remember?

MUM: Oh. *(Pause.)* You girls had so many songs.

Snow falls on them. The recorder chorus fades out.

End of Play

Thank you in the hugest ways to these people who are inspiring collaborators and amazing friends: Jess Barbagallo, Eliza Bent, Becca Blackwell, Enver Charkartash, Emily (Emily) Davis, Chris Giarmo, Erin Markey, Julia Sirna-Frest, and Susie Sokol. And to Zack Tinkelman, Andreea Mincic, Nathan Lemoine, Liz Nielsen, and Randi Rivera, who made the hustle to create these and other plays feel so worth it.

Tina Satter is a Brooklyn-based writer and director who makes plays, performances, videos, and music. She is Artistic Director of the theater company Half Straddle founded in 2008 and awarded an Obie grant in 2013. Her recent critically acclaimed show, *House of Dance*, about a transgender tap student, opened in October 2013 commissioned by Richard Maxwell's New York City Players and named a New York Times Critics Pick. Her play, *Seagull (Thinking of you)*premiered at PS122's 2013 COIL Festival following residencies at MASS MoCA, New Museum, and Abrons Art Center. It tours to France and Croatia in fall 2013 and spring 2014. Her play *In the Pony Palace/FOOTBALL* was named a Top 10 Show of 2011 by PAPER Magazine, among other honors, and *FAMILY* was named a Top 10 show of 2009 by *Time Out New York*. Her work has been curated into seasons at The Kitchen, PS122, Incubator Arts Project, the Bushwick Starr, Prelude Festival, and Ice Factory Festival. Her play *Away Uniform* had its European premiere at Culturgest in Lisbon, Portugal in October 2013.

Tina was named a "2011 Off-Off Broadway Innovator to Watch" by *Time Out New York*, was a 2013 Kitchen L.A.B. resident, and featured director at Culture Project's 2011 Women Center Stage Festival. She has been a guest artist and teacher at Princeton University, Reed College, and Fordham University. Tina attended Mac Wellman's graduate playwriting program at Brooklyn College and received a B.A. in English from Bowdoin College and an M.A. in Liberal Studies from Reed College.

FAMILY

Premiered in 2009 at the Ontological-Hysteric Theater

Written and Directed by Tina Satter

Music Composition and Sound Design by Chris Giarmo

Lighting Design by Zack Tinkelman

Set Design by Nathan Lemoine

Costume Design by Normandy Sherwood

Stage Management by Wayne Petro

Original cast:

Frarajaca	Erin Markey
Lily	Emily Davis
Mum (Agnes)	Rae C Wright
Rolf	Joseph Keckler
Bronstein	Eliza Bent
Sharon	Julia Sirna-Frest
Cygon	Katherine Scharhon
Phillipa	Sara Lindsay Copeland
Sharky	Chris Giarmo

Thank you to Shannon Sindelar, Brendan Regimbal, and Samara Naeymi for curating and supporting this project. To Rae C Wright for rehearsal space at N.Y.U., to Andre Callot for documenting the work, and Dr. Pearl Herbert for sanity.

Away Uniform

Premiered in 2012 at the Incubator Arts Project

Written and Directed by Tina Satter

Music Composition and Sound Design by Chris Giarmo

Lighting Design by Zack Tinkelman

Set Design by Andreea Mincic

Original cast:

Jem	Jess Barbagallo
Farah	Emily Davis
Jayjay	Pete Simpson

Thank you to Jeso O'Neill, Michael De Angelis, Normandy Sherwood, Craig Flanagin, Helen Satter, Chris Masullo, Jamie Peterson, Andre Callot, Antje Oegel, Sam Goodman, Shannon Sindelar, Brendan Regimbal, Samara Naeymi, Judy and Richard Hampe, Kathy and Richard Satter, Dianne and David Jenkins, Anne Sears, and a host of generous donors without whom it would not have been possible.

Seagull (Thinking of you)

Premiered in 2013 at PS122's COIL Festival, at the New Ohio Theatre

Written and Directed by Tina Satter

Music Composition and Sound Design by Chris Giarmo

Lighting Design by Zack Tinkelman

Set Design by Andreea Mincic

Costume Design by Enver Chakartash

Make Up Design by Naomi Raddatz

Stage Management by Randi Rivera

Assistant Stage Management by Aldora Neal

Production Management by Liz Nielsen

Assistant Direction by Chip Rodgers

Original cast:

Nina	Emily Davis
Masha	Eliza Bent
Treplov	Jess Barbagallo
Trigorin	Becca Blackwell
Arkadina	Susie Sokol
Polina	Julia Sirna-Frest

Seagull (Thinking of you) was made possible with commissioning support from Performance Space 122 and the Jerome Foundation. Developed in residences at MASS MoCA, the New Museum, and Abrons Art. Early stages of the work were shown at the Prelude Festival in 2011.

Thank you to Travis Chamberlain, Jay Wegman, Vallejo Gantner, Amy Rogoway, Robert Lyons, Antje Oegel, Bobby McElver, Michael De Angelis, Maeve Lowe, Cristina Alfaiate, Caleb Hammons, Helen Shaw, Tom Coiner, Kate Marvin, Olga Okuneva, Maxim Tumenev, John Wyszniewski, Jeso O'Neill, and Ilan Bachrach; the incredible residencies and their staffs; and again, a number of extraordinary people who donated to this show and made it possible to happen at all.

Cover photographs: Michael De Angelis
Character makeup drawings for *Seagull*: Naomi Raddatz
Book design: Karinne Keithley Syers
Printed on recycled paper.

53rd State Press publishes new writing for performance. It was founded in 2007 and is co-edited by Karinne Keithley Syers and Antje Oegel. For more information or to subscribe, visit 53rdstatepress.org. 53rd State Press books are distributed to the trade by Theatre Communications Group, through Consortium.

53SP 01 The Book of the Dog
53SP 02 Joyce Cho Plays
53SP 03 Nature Theater of Oklahoma's No Dice
53SP 04 Nature Theater of Oklahoma's Rambo Solo
53SP 05 When You Rise Up
53SP 06 Montgomery Park, or Opulence
53SP 07 Crime or Emergency
53SP 08 Off the Hozzle
53SP 09 A Map of Virtue and Black Cat Lost
53SP 10 Pig Iron: Three Plays
53SP 11 The Mayor of Baltimore and Anthem
53SP 12 Ich, KürbisGeist and The Secret Death of Puppets
53SP 13 Soulographie: Our Genocides
53SP 14 Life and Times: Episode 1
53SP 15 Life and Times: Episode 2
53SP 16 Life and Times: Episodes 3&4
53SP 17 The 53rd State Occasional No. 1
53SP 18 Seagull (Thinking of you) with Away Uniform and FAMILY